The Cognitive Rampage

The Cognitive Rampage

A scientific approach to self discovery, change and optimization

Adam Lowery MHC

Second Edition: 2017

ISBN: 1530236886
ISBN 13: 9781530236886
Library of Congress Control Number: 2016903235
CreateSpace Independent Publishing Platform
North Charleston, South Carolina

CONTENTS

DEDICATION

This book is dedicated to my daughter, Morgan Elise Lowery. You are the most authentic person I have known in my life. You are my peace. You are my greatest influence. You are my reason. I love you just the way you are and will be. Thank you for teaching me every day. May your future be what you make it and all that you have dreamed. I live my days with you forever in my heart and take you with me in my spirit eternally.

FOREWORD

I wrote this book for those seeking a scientific approach to life enhance-ment, experiencing a life change or want to create one. For those want-ing to cultivate and reveal their authentic selves. For those willing to question everything, and even for those who are unwilling. If your life is your passion (or if you want it to be), if you have even the slightest heartbeat left to rampage against your dark or push your light further, this is for you. If you believe in the power of the individual, or want to, this is for you. This is for the unique hopefuls who have refused to resign to *supposed to*. Those who know there are many ways and many paths. If you don't identify with any of these perspectives, then simply read for the experience. Sometimes the most life-altering moments occur during the most random experiences—many times experiences we initially avoided. These unpredictable moments of being suddenly uncomfortable can, in a moment, change your life. The constructively uncomfortable experiences reward you the most. Reading this may be one of those experiences. It will dose your present path with authentic moments and experiences you will start creating. That's right; you won't be watching and waiting for them to happen. You will craft the authentic moments and life experiences that will be your story. You are the author.

This approach is not going to show you the way, so to speak. I am not promising you will find happiness. You will create that if you choose. I am not asking you to find yourself either. I am asking you to simply use your-self. Go look in the mirror right now. There you are. Now that you have found yourself, it is time to use yourself. I am not guaranteeing sobriety and that all of your dreams will come true. That is up to you. This is the story of how I changed my life. This is what continues to grow my life daily. This approach has assisted others in doing the same. It was they who convinced me to write this down for others. It is you who will change your life.

In the simplest terms, this approach offers a framework for change and a path for steadfast growth. It is a framework I built from the pages of my revealing journal which documents all my life's most difficult transitions and then applying my academic study and my clinical experiences as a mental health practitioner. *The Cognitive Rampage* is a culmination of nearly twenty years of journaling and composing, integrated with my academic and personal study of historic and modern-day researchers, practitioners, philosophers and theorists. This approach also includes the wisdom of my life's most influential mentors' and their mentors. My academic study was fueled by my personal dedication to change my own life. Daily, I fed my passion for psychology, sociology, philosophy and mental and physical health—to gain the competencies I needed to change. In sum, it is how I changed my life and continue to dose it daily. I know this will help you do the same. In the end, it is still merely my perception of my own meandering in this wildly amazing moment we call the human experience.

You are writing your life story and each page is filled with the choices you make. The best part is, because you are writing the script, you control what happens next. When you can learn to think rationally, begin making choices from a rational place of optimistic possibility, learn to enthusiastically feed your mind, body and Spirit daily with knowledge, wisdom and experience, you will begin to cultivate and live purposefully. You won't have to find purpose; purpose will find you.

PHASE I: THE BACKGROUND, SCIENTIFIC INFLUENCE, AND STRATEGY

CHAPTER 1

THE HUMAN BEHIND THE RAMPAGE

I have my moments.

I have kept my journal since I was fifteen. Sometimes I would write poetry and sometimes just a question. I even drew sketches. I don't know why I wrote in this journal as though I was telling a story to someone; I don't even know who that someone was. I wrote descriptive statements and asked enraged questions in multiple tones and narratives. I did not realize till much later in life that I had unknowingly and vividly tracked my most influential life experiences and transitions from beginning to end. The fearful, angry, typical, and not-so-typical life transitions and experiences seemed to be the only times I would write in my journal. Imagine that. I began as a kid writing about my verbally, emotionally, and sometimes physically abusive father. I watched a strong and Spiritual man collapse from the pressures of this world. Endless nights of yelling, my mother's screams followed by sounds of something other than my heartbreaking under the fear of him. I have never been so scared of a hall light shining under my door and what was to come in the morning or when he got home from work. I never knew when or what was to come for most of my childhood. It was this state of constant fear that became the emotional terrorism that rippled for years in my life choices. I scribed my transition from fearing the very man who had enforced his every perception into my life, to being the only one around to tackle him from reaching the .357 Smith and Wesson revolver because he had enough of the pain and suddenly planned to end it all because my mother had left, again. Ironically, it was the same revolver I had played Russian roulette with at least half a dozen times from age twelve to about fourteen or fifteen. Although, today I credit him for planting a Spiritual seed, and my mother for cultivating it to its present strength. Through my journal, I could almost relive these weekly occurrences. My journal also included my transitions from a high school football player to a college player with NFL dreams, the dream-ending injury and the route to my life of crime. It was all there in my horrible public-school handwriting, spelling and grammar.

Later, as I began my education in mental health, I poured through the words in my journal not really knowing what to expect. I remember finding when addiction began to grab a hold. It was in my early twenties as I was forced out of football. I found a way to recapture the exhilaration I found in sports in the *dope game* and running nightclubs. Imagine that. The journal detailed all the adventure candy, drama and close calls that came with the lifestyle. But no names. My journal was riddled with nightmares, failures, and too much regret and shame to list here. I seemed to be passionately and constantly pissed off, focused solely on the pain of my life. I cynically concentrated on what was not right about my life: what wasn't fair, what should've happened. I was angry at what was supposed to have happened, what could've been.

The words also revealed the few successes in similar detail. Literary tracking of my experiences put in slow motion years of wide-ranging beliefs, thoughts and emotions. Each written thought hosted its own taste of memory, sour, bitter and sweet. Scribbles of arranged letters revealed my altering attitudes, bleak outlook and jaded beliefs. Now, with psychological training, I could see how each entry painted the exact picture the ugliness my words proposed. The beauty of emerging from each transitional experience was transcribed meticulously as well. I could see clear and present dialogue shifts; the verbiage that led me into further chaos and confusion and some that led me to be more alive than ever—*alive* meaning it read as though I was no longer willing to only survive but curious, even anxious, to grow.

I would title this journal *My Spiritual Rampage* at the end of a two-year journey I call my walkabout. The choice to leave on this walkabout was in no way planned and came after a night of sudden and unplanned life contemplation. I know how it sounds. Maybe it was spiritual contemplation. I still don't quite know what it was. There was no catalyst event to this typical night either. The name stuck, though. *My Spiritual Rampage* is now a phrase interchangeable between my lifelong journal and my roughly two-year walkabout. That random night of contemplation began my life's most uncomfortable journey.

I will try to summarize my walkabout because that adventure is a book unto itself, and this book is about you not me. My dream of football destroyed by injury, I became quickly and many times deeply involved in criminal activities, camouflaged by my work in the nightclub scene. At 22, I had been placed in inpatient detainment because it had been determined I was a threat to others and suicidal. If they had only known the truth of it. I had attempted a few relationships but pretty much was the ruin to most of those. They were all filled with drama, just like my home life had been. However, the relationship before embarking on my walkabout was the match to my gasoline. We reframed our drama as passion, but our relationship was actually quite destructive to us, to our health, our futures but also to our friendships and our families.

By the time I was 26, I had managed not to overdose or do any major prison time, just minimal jail time. I had, but some miracle, negotiated my exit from the drug business and become fully immersed in the nightclub business. When you move as much product as I was, *they* don't just let you walk away. At least at the moment, I owed no one, business was legal and going decently well. I was surprised I actually made it out of the *dope game* alive; I didn't see that happening because that was not my plan. Some friends were not so lucky. Both lifestyles, drugs and nightclub life, had intertwined and then come unwound. It had been a wild ride to say the least.

The day I left on my walkabout I was running a nightclub with ownership nights, and deep into plans of launching a new website venture. I was using cocaine and ecstasy much less often since I quit dealing it in such large quantities. Drinking was typically nightly and comes with *the business* if you let it. My all-nighters were down to a few times a week rather than days at a time. The nightclub business was as competitive, ruthless and unpredictable as the drug business. Running a successful one meant your club had to be the hottest, the newest, the sexiest place to be seen. There was good money to be made but success rested on what happened two to three nights a week. It was a constant hustle. As long as I had money, everything was OK. But living the nightclub life means I also spent it quickly. It all seemed just part of the business, part of the lifestyle, just *who I was*.

It was a typical weekday night. I was home early from the club. I had not done any synthetic drugs in a few weeks or so. It was around 3:00 a.m. and I sat down to smoke my usual blunt of California's finest to wind down. Except this time, it just didn't feel right. My thoughts were pulling me to analyze my past, my ruthless violence toward others, and especially what I did for a living, beyond the velvet ropes, the fun, the money, the ego. Is this it? Was I happy? An internal debate ensued for nearly sixteen hours in my living room. I placed the song *Epiphany* by Stained on repeat for some reason. Trust me; I know how this sounds. The thought and the question were now repeating. *Walk away from it all. Walk away from it all?* This toiling would continue through tears, anger, meditation, prayer and writing. This is who I was: Adam, or *Mike Lowery* as they called me, *the nightclub guy with hookups to anything and everything you want and need.*

Within two days of this night's end I had given away all I did not need, left my hard-earned career, all my plans and all my friends. In the middle of the night, I drove to the Florida Keys seeking purpose. I found humility. This was where I first learned that you have to be willing to get a uncomfortable to get healthy. I took a job working construction at the end of the summer heat, digging and filling holes in the limestone of a military runway just north of Key West, Florida. I slept in a house with four other guys doing the same labor work. My bed was a corner on a linoleum floor with couch cushions and a blanket. I spent more time on the job and in the gym than I did on that floor. I wanted nothing to do with the ego, night lights, velvet ropes, endless cocaine talk of business plans to get richer than the other guy and the continuous comparisons of each other's cars, homes, clothes and *craziest nights*. I was finished with any type of façade. Including my own. When I wasn't digging holes, painting or demolishing in potential asbestos, I was lifting, reading, writing, fishing or running. It is amazing what physical labor and nature can do for the mind, body, and Spirit. My life had been ego-driven till then, based in soulless choices chasing dark thrills, pretending it was for money, hiding behind the *do what you got to do* phrase you may know well. Like a tornado on an unknown path, I had been spinning violently since leaving the game I loved so much. I had been chasing the rush, the feelings of the Friday night lights and Saturday cheers ever since I had left them behind. Although the nightmares that began in my teens continued well into my twenties.

The long days of mind-numbing work allowed seemingly endless time for self- and life-reflection. With each passing workday, I began to contemplate, more and more, feelings of empathy for those I had harmed and those who had hurt me. It is hard to feel genuine empathy for those who harm us. I have come to believe wholeheartedly this is where you start. Who I was and who I was supposed to be melted away in the Florida Keys sun with each hole I dug, page I wrote and read, fish I caught, run I took and weight I lifted. Even though I don't lift weights anymore, it was helping me at the time. We will get to that later in the book.

After the Keys, I took off to Chattanooga, Tennessee to be closer to my brother and his family. Davy was the one who hooked me up with the Keys escape. He has, and continues to be there right when I need him most. Living near them would be the first time I would experience the idea of family in any healthy sense. I started to gain perspective on my life just by being around my young niece Seneca so often. I will never forget our first uncle and niece breakfast. There was something reassuring watching my powerful niece play in nature, and places where people still say *Ma'am*. That time with my brother and his family fed my humbling spirit with real joy. It wasn't perfect and neither was I. I almost relapsed into the club business when I was tempted by a quick-fix, easy-money nightclub project. I had not touched any synthetics weeks before embarking. I did attempt a relationship before I was healthy, but, predictably, I ruined that one as well.

A trip set up once again through my brother and his contacts out West gave me a chance to experience life on the Reservation in New Mexico, what many refer to as *The Rez*. That trip quickly put a stop to every relationship and another club takeover, both near and potentially very emotionally lucrative mistakes.

While on the Rez, I had many powerful Spiritual experiences. One day I chose to walk down an ancient path from atop a mountain flat, a flat hosting a Native American burial ground, a site just off the steps of one of the oldest churches in this country. The burial ground ran to the edge of a deep canyon full of soaring, diving, and gliding ravens and crows—at least a hundred. The sky immediately above seemed to be the only space the birds would soar. It is the most powerful view I have ever seen to date in my life. The walk from there down to the valley was when one of these powerful and affecting moments occurred. The path I was walking down was the path the Apache used to bring up water and food to the flat. They had to move from the lush valley for better protection from the invading US government. This path was kept hidden by natural camouflage in the twists and turns of the steep run down. I paused for a moment when a distance view broke from the rocky walled path overlooking a mountain in the distance. I thought of both of my grandfathers and just listened to Nature. The details of this and the many other moments I choose to keep private. That experience and many others like it changed my life perceptions. That moment on the path down I stopped forcing my past life experiences to define who I was. It was no longer my truth. I admitted I did not know who I was. I began to question myself, the world, and others with an empathetic openness, appreciation, and a humbled curiosity for knowledge, wisdom and understanding. I returned to Florida at twenty-nine years old, nearly two years after my sudden departure. My life would never be the same. Who I was and who I am were no longer present. My belief canvas had been wiped clean.

I started coaching at the YMCA in their youth flag football league. In two seasons, those little men did more for me then I am sure any of my coaching did for them. More than any therapy session had ever done for me, past and present. I had no other true place to call home except the gym I frequented, a few friends' couches or an '89 Tahoe I purchased from my uncle. I pursued pastoral school briefly but quickly came to the belief that neither I nor anyone could hold any such monopolized seat or claim some exclusive right to infuse the Book with so much personal interpretation. No offense. For lack of better or more authentic terms, my Spiritual life was different than religion had ever taught me it was supposed to be when I was a child. It was more honest.

I had left a business after nearly a decade of focus. I was starting over at 29 with no dope money stash, no savings account, no assets, no 401(k), an entrepreneur and nightclub résumé, no credit, no home and no plan. I had liquidated self inside and out. I only knew I wanted to live differently and maybe help people one day. With my football training experience, I began personal training for peanuts at the gym I frequented because it had helped me so much. Although I no longer lift, it was my physical fuel at the time. Plus, I spent so much time there as it was. I would train others and work on some side ideas when I could put down a barbell, book, or coaching clipboard. This was also the first time I would be invited to speak in public. A high school friend set me up to speak to athletes at our old middle school about being leaders because they were athletes. I ended up changing it to *Why they should help others learn to become better athletes.* I prepped for almost two weeks for a 15-minute speech to middle-school students. That day changed my life.

The personal training was barely covering the bills, but I was happier than I had ever been in my life. I was eating better than I had ever eaten in my life. I was a workout and reading machine. I finally read a book my mother had given me years earlier after leaving inpatient treatment at twenty-two years old. I use to regret not reading it the moment she gave it to me. I am also happy I never gave it away. I can never seem to hold on to a book I love because I give it away to someone I think might need it. The book was *A Guide to Rational Living* by Dr. Albert Ellis. I think the speech I gave that day, terrified in front of middle-school kids, and this book, seeded the eventual push to my present-day professional life. I had become vulnerable and compassionate, no longer focused on the pain and regret, but the human potential. Vulnerable but focused this time on the competence I was gaining by being more aware and humbly curious, not focused on the pain of what was, or should be. I was now beginning to paint on my blank canvas new beliefs about the world, others, and myself. Reading that book was a cognitive experience for me like no other. I enjoyed this experience and the life-changing experiences of many other books many times. I still do. Each book offered a different human experience. Each sentence provided a peak into more self-competence and possibility. Not to mention provided strategies and tools. Reading these multiple experiences fed a growing enthusiasm. The last of my once concrete life seemed to crumble away naturally.

The more I read psychology, philosophy and related research, the more enthusiastic I became about my own life, the more confident I became that I could help others. My mother had planted a seed many years ago with a book, a competence seed. This once tiny interest had been developing into a competence, fed by my hunger for learning as much as I could. Gaining competence in my areas of interest had now grown into an enthusiastic way of life. As I read others' written accounts of their life experiences, thoughts, and philosophies, my curiosity, passion, and enthusiasm grew. An unquenchable thirst for the optimistic possibilities drove my desire for self-competence. Peace was real in my life for the first time. I was feeling humbly confident while having no future plan, being the most financially destroyed I had ever been and being early in this transition, still quite alone. My thoughts constantly reminded me I only knew what I know now because I admitted I knew nothing first. If that was to continue, then the practice of humility needed to be on the forefront of my days. Like a watermark, it needed to be stamped over everything I learned, felt and thought. The moment I stop being humble in my learning and my teaching, I risk a detour that could destroy all the gains I have made.

I continued to study all the theoretical foundations of psychology and as many historical, current, and emerging theories and therapies as I could sniff out or had heard about in passing. I was doing this as though my life depended on it. I was enthusiastic to say the least. First, I had to learn for myself, my personal *whats* and *whys*. I was looking for the *how to* for *changing* my life and eventually helping others do the same.

Deciding to pursue my master's in mental health counseling was no difficult choice with my new outlook and Life Philosophy. I didn't study. I trained relentlessly, like it was two-a-day football camp. I researched, questioned, wrote, and read like it was a race to save lives, including my own. I still do. I studied theories and read books not required by the classes on top of the required material. I dove deep into self-analysis at the same time. I still do. I now say my student loans are probably the amount therapy would have cost me to get to where I am in my life currently, but I did it in half the time. That thought makes me feel better when the student loan bill comes every month.

After returning from my walkabout and completing my master's in mental health counseling, I began to cultivate what I call my Cognitive Rampage; a daily enthusiastic but humble questioning of self, others, and the world. Cultivating an enthusiasm for self and life through daily feedings of competence in mind, body and belief. To create experiences and not wait for them. I have worked hard to live my life this way since returning from my walkabout. I still do.

By the time I was 31, I had married and officially became a father to the most authentic person I know, Morgan Elise Lowery. By the end of year three of my return, I had completed my master's in mental health counseling and graduated with near perfect scores. I was even hired as a full-time Clinical Therapist in a dual diagnosis hospital while still finishing my internship. My new beliefs, Life Philosophy and daily structure led me to find a real and honest relationship with myself, experience unconditional love for someone else for the first time in my life and purpose found me seemingly overnight. It had taken me roughly 25 years to get where I was before I departed on my Spiritual Rampage, but only about five years to change my life to something I had never imagined possible. Getting out of the hole doesn't take as long as it took you to get in there. But it does if you believe it to.

I am now sure I could not have experienced and begun living my Cognitive Rampage had I not experienced my first Spiritual Rampage. Had I not embraced and experiences the darkness that was my past, I may not have accepted my Spiritual Rampage.

Darkness can cause destruction, but it also breeds creation.

My experiences from the therapist's chair continued to feed a passion that I ate, slept and spoke of 24/7. I spoke with dedicated enthusiasm and a humbled confidence. I wanted to help everyone I could using the new *whats* and *whys* I had learned in my study, my travels and life experiences.

I studied many amazing new theories, research, treatments and competencies. Many of these approaches have shown much promise and more positive outcomes then what is typically practiced. Today, new and emerging theories and approaches and are rarely used inside walls of Medicare and Medicaid-funded facilities, not because they are not effective but because they are not reimbursable. Practitioners are often held within the confines of the 12 Step approach. It's the same as it was 13 years ago, when I was a patient; nothing had changed. The program hadn't worked for me; they didn't even teach the 12 Step approach in my master's program. Still I had to stick to the steps, this time from the therapist's chair. The steps approach works for many people. The research varies from 5% to 25% recovery rates. This is not my argument. It is helping the other 75% to 95% of people struggling with this one size-fits all approach. In my opinion it is unethical that we know such a large percentage will fail and we simply blame them, a disorder or *disease*. Especially because we have an ethical responsibility to offer any and all available possibilities of help and treatment, but cannot due to legal corruption. It is a waste of humanity. I am a supporter of the 12 Steps, but it cannot be the only or main offered approach today. This is my argument. I support what works for the individual. If the 12 Steps, Alcoholics Anonymous and/or Narcotics Anonymous works for you, then I am cheering you on to the next step. It should continue to be an offered approach. How can we continue to ignore a large percentage of human beings and simply act as though they just are not applying themselves?

I must also note that synthetic medication was almost always a part of the treatment program. Pharmacological intervention is more easily provided, billed and reimbursed. At a minimum, this approach ensured the return of these patients shortly after their release from their time-limited treatment. The treatment prescribed at these facilities is driven by what the insurance companies will pay for, not by doctors and therapists using all rational means available to help someone who is in desperate need of their help. The more competent I became as a therapist, the more I could see a failing system perpetuating and even creating more pain and suffering.

The time spent working in a government-funded dual-diagnosis treatment centers changed the path of my life dramatically, although not at all in the way I envisioned. My idealism quickly collided with the reality that the treatment center was more pawn than king in this game; it could not survive without revenue from the insurance companies, US tax dollars and corrupt legislation. They were the real power in this scheme. Taking down the power of insurance companies is like deciding to fight the rising tide. You can spend a lot of time, money and energy to slow the tide, but it is a force of nature that won't be denied until the masses decide enough is enough. That's not to say I would give in and join the team or give up and walk away. I had to say and eventually do something.

With the counsel of my Primary Mentor, Leo D'Anniballe, I began to explore and build an approach that would be not only scientifically based, but provide meaningful, lasting change. First, I would begin to speak out about the depth of the corrupt mental health system, the corrupt legalities and protocols linked to insurance companies that decided on treatment approaches and time frames. When profit drives these decisions, we are left with the cheapest, quickest (and often stalest) treatments. But it wasn't enough to protest, reveal and press for restructuring our health care system. I wanted to carve out a different path for people to change their lives. I did not want to focus on selected symptoms like addiction or depression.

I hunted for a proactive path that would lead to dynamic changes on all fronts simultaneously: cognitive, behavioral, environmental and biological. How I changed my life was recorded in my journal but was revealed through my training.

Leo offered more than 30 years of combined clinical research, private and clinical practice as a licensed clinical social worker and facility director. He offered guidance and mentorship in nearly every word. I had a much different life experience to offer. I too, had clinical experience, but from both chairs, and enough academia to numb anyone's Spirit. My vigor for the art of helping fueled my seemingly endless quest to optimize an approach people could apply in their life that did not call for pills and powerlessness. During endless nights for the next three years I relived my life experiences through my journal and cultivated new competencies. I'd build. I'd tear down and rebuild again. Like John Nash in his quest for an original idea, tirelessly I moved the pieces around. The culmination, refining, and polishing of these pieces revealed what I call Transrational Structural Behavior Theory, or TSBT.

Trans- is a prefix occurring in loanwords from Latin *to transcend* or *change thoroughly*. On the TSBT model it is used in combination with elements of the *Rational* origin. *Transrational* means to transition to a rational thinking process and self-talk. This requires more than simple cognitive reframing, but deep belief extraction. Beliefs that are processed through rational filters and applied behaviorally in a personalized structure for quicker affect and assimilation. This combines a structured behavioral approach with the cognitive sciences while also accounting for environmental and biological influences.

TSBT is also a culmination of my past life of living in a literal rampage, my Spiritual Rampage, and my present life experience. *Transrational Structural Behavior Theory* just sounded like so many other relatively confusing theories, got to be a mouth full and sounded so pretentious when I heard myself say it. This approach needed to be different. It is how the *Cognitive Rampage* was born: a literal *thinking rampage; a targeted destruction of all existing irrational notions of truth and reality by mindfully observing self exploration and revealing the self through a humble questioning of self, others and the world. To live daily with a passionate curiosity for competence in order to cultivate an enthusiasm for creating life experiences* -simply put, *to live your Cognitive Rampage!*

Perhaps nothing truly is original. We build upon one another in this life. This is a building block carved out of my life experience set for others to build, grow, and tear apart, just as I did to create the Cognitive Rampage approach to mastering life's transitions and cultivating personal revelations. This was my dose of authentic revelation I now offer to you. There are no harmful side effects.

CHAPTER 2

COMPETENCE CREATORS

The possibility of flight was once an impossibility…until it wasn't.

This simple statement by Aubrey De Gray captures all the possibilities of human potential. Amazing discoveries happen almost daily. The capability and capacity of humans seems infinite. To Aubrey and all of my mentors mentioned in this chapter and throughout this book, and those who are not, thank you for painting your life experiences unapologetically with the most authentic strokes. Thank you for being fearlessly who you authentically are. To my readers, open yourself up to possibilities fearlessly. Expand your own beliefs, but be willing to tear them down too. Your life may depend on it.

To examine yourself, you need know what to look for, you need to understand what makes you who you are now. It does not necessarily mean you need to spend hours *on the couch*, randomly reviewing thoughts, feelings and experiences. This too is a circle you can find yourself lost within. I believe we can target those beliefs that most define you. But most importantly, it is not so much *what* you review as *how* you review those influences. I will ask you to examine your beliefs, your life experiences and your external environments, both past and present, as you duel within the collage of your present internal environment. In looking at your beliefs, I will ask you to consider what you believe to be true, how you process information and your self-talk. Your internal environment includes your biological and genetic design, history and functioning. Your external environment is important because the experiences you have had with people, places and things have created your perception of reality. Your perceived reality shapes how you process information. The internal and external environments continually challenge each other. Your biological, genetic and neurological development and present functioning have been (and continue to be) shaped by your experiences and your experiences have been filtered through your biological, genetic and neurological functioning.

I believe it is this *cocktail* of variables affecting you at varying moments and degrees throughout your life that makes you who you are, how you are and why you are. This may sound like the nature-versus- nurture debate. But I believe it is much more complex; it is nature and nurture and more. Simply stated, all the key variables perpetually impact your current state of being. These perceptions are strong enough to concretely shape who you believe yourself to be and who you will become in the future. It is not important to me to find a formula for determining how much each of these variables impacts us. It is more important for you to discover what variables seem to have impacted you the most. How many authentic moments over a lifetime can potentially impact your internal environment to create the infinite combinations that become the ever-changing you, *the individual?* Recognizing the limitless combinations, can we really define the individual in concrete or subjective terms: *This is who I am. This is what I believe and this is what is truth.*

We all may experience similar situations, issues and moments in life. But we cannot experience life exactly the same way as someone else, even if we tried. To think so is arrogance. We are not all wired the same. Life did not give us all the exact moments and exact experiences especially at the exact same times in our lives. Since we are not wired the same, we do not experience life the same even in similar situations with similar context. It is nearly impossible to be the same. This is why it may feel as though no one has ever understood you. It is because they cannot. Your own beliefs about yourself, your experiences, others, the world and truth will change over time. That same process happens for everyone. The possibilities for differences in beliefs at any point in time are infinite.

Dr. Bruce Lipton, author of *The Biology of Belief*, surrounds the power of the belief with more potency than I have heard to date. One of my favorite of his examples, is about a mother's love for her child. A mother has picked up a car before to save her child. How could this happen? Adrenaline does not make us superheroes. But do you think for one second this mother thought she could not pick up the car?

I love this notion because the seemingly impossible was just that, until it wasn't. This speaks to the power of the belief, a foundation for your Cognitive Rampage; accept that what you believe to be true and not true in its entirety about any given moment, in any given moment, possible or impossible at any given time, may not be true. My simple approach to the notion of impossible is this. If you are not willing to talk about the impossible, then you are planning for the inevitable. Accepting the power of your beliefs is the most important first step you can take. Understanding that your beliefs are biologically linked to your past and present is essential. For this reason, I want to provide a brief overview of some important new concepts in science. This is not provided merely to provide information but to also to potentially challenge some of your existing beliefs or knowledge. These are very brief summaries of in-depth science. I invite you, if you are interested or if you are doubtful, to explore and investigate and examine as I did. It will change you.

Dr. Rhonda Patrick: Life Extension in Practice

The knowledge of what your body is doing, will most likely do and needs to function properly, if turned into action, will help you forecast your future and prevent much suffering. Dr. Rhonda Patrick, a leading biomedical scientist, provides new scientific platforms with her research and voice. Her colleagues and fellow researchers share and build on one another's discoveries. Dr. Patrick freely reveals her research and insights from years of concentration on the best ways to increase your life span. She provides many scientific and organic methods to protect the health of your body and mind. Her research linking nutrition, vitamin D, gut bacteria, head trauma and brain functioning to mood, mind and body function is life extension in practice. Breakthrough research and new revelations are emerging consistently from Dr. Patrick and her colleagues. They are revealing hope with their work; hope because this research brings medical and mental health, scientific research and nutrition together.

Epigenetics

Dr. Patrick and another Virtual Mentor quoted at the beginning of this chapter, Dr. Aubrey De Gray, are authors and biomedical gerontologists. Both work in the emerging and dynamic field of epigenetics. Even though epigenetics is founded on some paradigm-shifting discoveries and principles, I will use a brief speech given by another Virtual Mentor, philosopher and Competence Creator, Jason Silva. His *Shots of Awe* approach to explaining epigenetics is a shining example of delivering a Cognitive Rampage. I believe this speech to be an experience whether read, heard or seen. He leaves you excited and wanting more knowledge, more understanding, more possibilities.

Jason Silva: *There is a lifelong debate, the nature-versus-nurture debate. Are we prewritten beings? Are we predetermined? Do our genetics dictate our fate or are we made by our environment, molded by our experiences? Does language structure how we see the world? Does culture dictate who we become? Are we molded and shaped by the unfolding dynamics of interfacing with our environments? This is known as epigenetics. Literally, things that happened to you in your formative years can transform how your genetic structure is expressed. Experience can change biology. In recent debate and cited from The Social Life of Genes, the explanation that epigenetics goes much further in that experience, throughout our lives, actually effects our genetic expression. I have used the quote by a doctor researching epigenetic influence that 'ourselves or our bodies are a technology that turns experience into biology.' Even the cognitive framing that we give to experiences can change the physical expression of our cellular biology. So that, consciousness itself, interpretation, storytelling and framing, how we give meaning to our lives, can actually have a real effect at our genetic level; the way our genetic software expresses itself. We all have seen the bumper stickers stating the power of the mind and the power of positive thinking, the fact that we can shape our reality. But this notion does not just effect genetic expression at one point in our lives, but throughout our lives. It means that we are constantly composing our own biological unfolding. 'I design, therefore I become.' This is the power of experience on your now.*

Thank you for that Jason Silva.

The Brain

Mind and body improvement, optimization and extension is not just a multi-billion-dollar business. Most importantly, it is one of the fastest growing areas of science. We are learning to prevent disease, create active healing and extend life through improved cognition, nutrition, movement and the study of biological and genetic variance. Emerging research and new technologies, such as brain mapping and imaging, neurofeedback, frequency stimulation and neurotrophics are changing lives. I believe we are still in our infancy in the true understanding of the human species' most complicated, evolutionary and powerful tool: the brain.

Yet again, Dr. Patrick's voice and research on brain functioning, including history and treatment, are revealing the brain as potentially playing a starring role in shaping how you see the world and interact with it. If we are in our infancy in understanding the brain, then our understanding of brain trauma is an embryo. We know even the slightest brain disturbance or damage can be devastating. To ignore the brain in considering your development, would be naiveté in its most obvious form. Your brain may be the most powerful influence to who you are. Perhaps the answers to all your questions are locked in your brain waiting to be discovered.

Steven Kotler and Jamie Wheal: *Flow State*

Does our brain master us or do we master our brain? Does it generate thought or simply act as a receiver, processor and organizer of information? Virtual Mentors Steven Kotler and Jamie Wheal Founders of the Flow Genome Project provide a wealth of knowledge relating to brain stimulation, functioning and optimization. Also known and defined as *Flow State*. I am still trying to catch up. As a freestyle poet since my teens, their work on flow states continues to pique my fascination. Steven and Jamie's new book *Stealing Fire* researches and details all we know, and don't know about *Flow*. This is a real life superhero power. There is so much left to be discovered, and like a child on his birthday, a eagerly await for more of Steven and Jamie's competence creations.

Hormones

There are more than 50 hormones circulating and secreting from you, all affecting you at various levels of functioning and development. Dr.

Mark L. Gordon is an expert on biological functioning. He is also a healer, researcher, game changer and Virtual Mentor I look to for competence regarding hormonal influences. His knowledge, research and daily practice centers around various hormonal balances that need to be adjusted, monitored and maintained. These balances are affected by traumatic experiences, poor nutrition, medications, possible genetic structure, and, most certainly, environmental impacts. Dr. Gordon has been a prominent advocate for this emerging research for years. He presently uses these treatment interventions for those suffering from severe post-traumatic stress disorder (PTSD), depression and even addiction. Dr. Gordon is changing and saving lives. He is reducing the overuse of synthetic interventions and, therefore, reducing overdoses. He is helping fight the *magic pill* epidemic and the standard addiction treatment process I call *chemical incarceration*. Dr. Mark Gordon is a competence creator.

Dr. Jack Kruse and Light

First off, there is no simple way to dumb down this man's life changing work, but I will attempt it in a very short disbursement. Blue light is killing you. Nature and sunlight heals you and cannot be substituted. Dr. Jack Kruse is a neurosurgeon, optimal health educator, and an innovator to say the least. His immense research on the various light effects on human health is shaking up the entire scientific community and changing lives. It will save yours to say the most. From our eyes to our finger tips and feet, our light absorbers and the types of light we are absorbing, and not, are causing our health to diminish at a rapid pace. We are surrounded by artificial lighting and environments full of life sucking energies. Environments devoid of our natural human needs. When I found Dr. Kruse's work, believe me I was thrown back, and not to mention could barely grasp the science to which he has so meticulously studied, currently writes and speaks about. Since installing just his basic concepts, *biohacks* and methodologies my life, not just physically, but mentally, began to move to a level to which even the most optimal nutrition and exercise could not create. Indeed, all matter on Earth is made of atoms, however all life on Earth are made of cells. Therefore to clarify, all living things including our bodies, are made up of cells, which are in turn made up of atoms. Atoms are made of electrons, protons and neutrons. We are made of light. The type of light you lose and absorb matters.

I am not a scientist, and as I promised earlier, I want to keep the discussion of science as an overview intended to challenge your thinking and perhaps spark your curiosity. I only recommend these Competence Creator's work and their voices as a place to find knowledge and, with that, amazing possibilities. These scientists, researchers, authors and educators are a few of my Virtual Mentors. Later, I will cover in more detail how important mentorship is in living your Cognitive Rampage.

I wanted to include this chapter because I am a believer in the value of science, both that which has been understood for centuries and that which is cutting-edge. I listen with a sense of optimistic possibility and pursue any newly acquired interest. I also did not want this book to sound as though nothing else affects your development and current state in life. I am not this naive. I am excited for what the future of science holds for our health and lifespan, and what that means for our enjoyment of life.

The emphasis on science in no way limits the Spiritual or religious forces. For some, their personal definition of *Spirit* is essential to their beliefs and motivations. The word *Spirit* is a vague word with broad subjectivity; it may also make some people uncomfortable. I use it to be inclusive and respectful. You may substitute this very nebulous word with your own specific word and meaning. Or you may consider it the essence of you or the tone of your life's narrative. Or don't use it at all, but this would not be my advice. Although, this is not a requirement of this organic prescription for change to be applied in our physical and conscious world. It is defined as you deem it in your life. Sometimes accepted science is found to be flawed or incomplete. It changes and grows just as our own knowledge and beliefs change and grow. The same may be said for the Spiritual.

CHAPTER 3

THE JOURNEY

To consistently change how you think, feel, and behave,
you must first change what you believe.
-LEO D'ANNIBALLE

There are four Principles of Change. The Principles of Change are the guides to change. Understand and practice these principles to explore self, others and the world. After these principles have been explained in detail, you will be given the Tools of Change to apply to the Components of Change. As you use the Tools of Change on the Components of Change, you will need to continue to refer back to the principles. These principles will warn you of roadblocks and even detours you are creating or taking because of unhealthy beliefs. They will also guide you through this journey and to consistent personal growth. Cultivating, refining and connecting these Principles, Tools and Components of Change will begin to reveal your authentic Cognitive Rampage.

I do not want to get too detailed or beyond the Principles or Tools of Change just yet, but I do want to give you the Components of Change so they are in your mind as you learn and interpret the Principles of Change: 1) Your Core Beliefs; 2) Biological: Nutrition, Movement and Sleep; 3) Current Diagnoses and Treatment - Only/If applicable; 4) Environments: Internal and External Beliefs; 5) The People, Places, and Things in your life and your 6) Authentic Routine. Change in these Components equals change on all fronts. Literally, the strongest human dose for change to date. Change created by you. All of you will be analyzed and reconstructed from your rational and optimistic place of truth, not emotion.

I urge you to use a notebook to write down or even draw your work, thoughts and experiences as you journey into living your Cognitive Rampage. Find a way to record it all down. Track your life as it transcends. As another Virtual Mentor of mine Joe Rogan loves to say, *Write it down!* There is a book hidden in your life. You and I both believe that. You will cultivate the authentic you the same way you got here, through your beliefs, thoughts, choices, behaviors, experiences and environmental interactions both internally and externally. The Components of Change are continued works in progress, just like you. What you cultivate in the beginning of this approach will likely not be the same by the time you complete the initial application. That's OK. Go back and change it. We are all a constant work in progress. The purpose here is to excavate you and then provide the foundation so that you may continue in your life, changing authentically as you go. If self-discovery, awareness, change, and continuous growth are what you are looking for, this may be the approach for you. I will ask you to push yourself to challenge all you believe to be true about the world, others, your past, present, future and, especially, who you are. Do not say *it is what it is*. It is what you make it. You are not just who you are. You are who you believe yourself to be.

Anything not growing is dead.
—Lauren Hill

PHASE II: THE PRINCIPLES OF CHANGE

KEEP THESE IN MIND THROUGHOUT THE APPLICATION OF THIS APPROACH AND IN LIFE.

CHAPTER 4

THE CORE BELIEFS PRINCIPLE

There is power in the plasticity of perception.

Your beliefs are what you have accepted to be true and what you have not. Have you ever analyzed your belief or truth? You might think I'm asking you to be Plato. But what if I'm asking you to be Play-Doh? Meaning, your truth is a matter of your philosophical perceptions. This is your most powerful Principle of Change: the power of your beliefs.

This is a double-edged sword. *In your greatest strength lies your greatest weakness,* my mother always told me. I have come to find this to be true. You are your greatest strength, and you are your greatest weakness. Your beliefs can propel your ability to grow and change. They can also seed prosperity. The beauty of this power is in its natural existence; its avail-ability to humans at most any time and its ability to manifest in your life outcomes over time. Likewise, your beliefs can be self-defeating. They can manifest in a negative attitude, poor choices and bad relationships. All this based in beliefs you may have never recognized or examined.

In order to harness the power of beliefs, you need to excavate your cur-rent beliefs; beliefs you hold to be factual truths without question. More specifically your *Core Beliefs; your beliefs about the world, others and yourself.* Every other belief is filtered through one or all of your Core Beliefs. If all you think filters through these three Core Beliefs and they are nega-tive, irrational and pessimistic, how might you think? How might you then feel? How might you then behave?

A *Concrete Belief* is a personal perception of truth. Truth is an indisputable fact, immune to the natural plasticity of human perception. Beliefs become accepted as truth because they are founded in past experiences, past experiences which become reinforced (and often altered) with ongoing internal and external dialogue. Your *Core Beliefs are your beliefs about the world, others and self.* If you listen closely, your Core Beliefs can be heard in your self-talk and your words about others and the world. Many times your dialogue holds hidden (and sometimes not-so-hidden) assumptions. These assumptions reflect expectations of the world, yourself and others, including your friends and family.

You can be so faithful to your Core and other concreted beliefs that you may not even realize you have been responding from them for most of your life. Not being aware of your Core and concrete beliefs naturally allows you to elude ever questioning them, as possibly being meticulously modified personal perceptions. That's counterintuitive. How could you grow and change as a person if you have never stated and examined your Core and concrete beliefs? Perhaps it's because it's hard and uncomfortable. Perhaps you just want to stay right?

Your beliefs perpetuate the tone of your present life's narrative, beliefs you have the power to change with perception reconstruction. You believe your perceptions to be truth because you lived it, as a participant or as a witness. That's why you are the only one who can evaluate and, if necessary, change your perceptions and your beliefs. They feel like facts because they are your experiences. Aren't all experiences subject to perception? And if your beliefs are unhealthy, if they are holding you back or hurting you and your relationships, then you can re-examine and modify or *reframe* your perceptions and change your beliefs. Your past experiences are what they are now because of your perception of them, a perception planted in concrete through meticulously chosen dialogue, dialogue heavily influenced by cultural and social constructs and personal expectations.

This may be hard to process and accept, but there is no truth in our conscious and physical world. To soon? What I mean is your beliefs are only your perceptions of truth. If that statement hit you like a sledgehammer, then you have just experienced how challenging a concrete belief can produce an immediate emotional reaction through a thought. This takes the simple act of reframing your dialogue to a much deeper level. You can simply *reframe* or change and modify your perception with more rational and optimistic dialogue, but this will not last nor eliminate the irrational perception from returning. Reframing is meant to reduce the impact, or stop the redlining of your emotional engine. Belief extraction requires a deeper level of analysis. Belief modification of your beliefs requires a sincere practice of humility, but will also adjust your emotional engine to run steady, consistently.

Maybe this will help illustrate this principle. If you ride a roller coaster and do not think it to be scary in the slightest: and If I ride the same roller coaster and say it was the scariest ride of my life, who is telling the truth? Truth and reality have plasticity in our mental and physical dimensions. Perhaps the ride made me physically ill or perhaps I was made to ride one when I was too young and was derided for being afraid. Perhaps I have knowledge of the mechanics of roller coasters and realize how quickly human error could send us over the edge. You, on the other hand, loved the feeling of exhilaration, it felt like you were flying and you have no interest in the mechanics or maintenance of roller coasters. So many factors influenced our experience (and hence our belief) about that roller coaster ride. Your beliefs are based on your perceptions of your experience on the roller coaster of life. These perceptions became your concrete beliefs because you lived or are living them. I mean, you rode that ride right? They are reinforced daily with dialogue and behavior and challenges to them are usually rejected forthwith.

You will excavate your *Core Beliefs: beliefs about self, others and the world* in the beginning steps of building your Life Philosophy in Chapter 9. Your three Core Beliefs are the foundations you lay all your other and more specific beliefs upon. Your Concrete Beliefs about your past, your future, your relationships, your capabilities, even your nutrition and exercise are fed by your Core Beliefs. These beliefs are the masterminds driving your thinking, which is why it is so important for us to spend time on them. It will be time well spent.

Most of your beliefs, your truths can be traced back to something overwhelmingly subjective. For some, trauma becomes motivation. For others, it becomes a cancer. Changing perception helps fight mental cancer.

Let's say you had two of you: A and B. Both are equal in your definition of happiness and success. A has faced no adversity, has been handed most things on a silver platter and experienced little to no resistance, failure or trial on the path to success. B lived your life, with its hurdles, roadblocks and disappointments and still achieved happiness and accomplishment. Who do you respect more? B? If you did, then be grateful you have experienced all you have experienced because that IS YOU! Remember *B-You* and say thank you to life for all the shit it has put you through.

> *There is power in the plasticity of your beliefs and perceptions. You are what you perceive yourself to be.*

CHAPTER 5

THE B-TO-B PRINCIPLE

This Principle of Change and much of this approach has been seasoned by and built from historical philosophers, cognitive psychologist, theorists and cognitive approaches and discoveries. Historical Empiricists such as Berkeley and Hume. The 19th Century minds of Wundt, Helmholtz, Titchener and James. The 20th Century gave us names such as Skinner, Lazarus, Kohler, Tolman, Bartlett and Chomsky to pull from. Cognitive-based therapeutic approaches were also utilized. Approaches such as Cognitive Behavioral Therapy (CBT) by Founder by Dr. Aaron Beck, and especially Dr. Albert Ellis, Founder of Rational Emotive (Behavior) Therapy (REBT/RET). These historical theorists and practitioners are still Virtual Mentors of mine. I pull from all of these Competence Creators life's work.

You can have a positive concrete belief or a negative concrete belief. A positive concrete belief begets optimistic thoughts, positive but rational thoughts you construct that shape positive feelings. A negative concrete belief can appear rational, but perpetuates pessimistic tones and negative thoughts used to reinforce personal perception. It is important to understand my meaning of the word *positive*. I mean this word as *inspiring, optimistic and constructive* to the growth of your life or others without causing harm. As I use the word, it also is structured rationally. You can safely assume *negative* to be the opposing definition. Understanding whether your concrete beliefs are positive or negative, you must also examine if they are rational. Many of our concrete beliefs were formed during our most influential years, rewarding and traumatizing experiences. Whether these beliefs are positive or negative, must be re-examined.

If you hold an unwavering or *concrete* positive belief about yourself, how might you speak to yourself about yourself? Again, the same question about the opposite. What thoughts and feelings are echoed from a negative concrete belief? More importantly, why would you hold on to negative beliefs that breed poisonous and often irrational thoughts? Why grasp so tightly to your concrete beliefs if the thoughts born from those beliefs create feelings you don't want to feel or promote behaviors you no longer wish to continue?

Your Concrete Beliefs, both positive and negative, are revealed in your thoughts. The outcome of your thoughts are your feelings. Most of us have either never examined our Concrete Beliefs or quit doing so a long time ago. But we do so at our own peril. It is our Concrete Beliefs that lay the foundation for everything we think and, therefore, everything we feel. And when we understand that our feelings generally predict behavior, we realize that our efforts to change have begun from the wrong starting line.

Feelings rise, often too quickly, from your automatic thoughts or thoughts that seem to just appear suddenly. Thoughts stemming from your positive and negative concrete beliefs, beliefs that have sprouted from your negative or positive Core Beliefs. Your feelings are then reinforced by your inner and outer dialogue. This purposefully-chosen dialogue enhances the feelings you think you should feel. Your thoughts create how you feel, not the moment, not the other person, not the experience. You do it all. Your thoughts are the gas to your matchbox of beliefs. Your feelings are often just the flames of your thoughts burning wildly in any direction without concern for surroundings. This is not intended to just describe someone who is outwardly out of control. These flames may be slow-burning, deliberate, calculating, even Machiavellian. What is important are not the outward signs but the basis for the behavior, the feelings and the thoughts. You perceive the moment, the person or environment through your beliefs. You then interpret these perceptions and create your thoughts. Your thoughts then create your feelings. Your feelings predict your behavior. But it all begins with your Core and concrete beliefs, both positive and negative. This is Principle #2: <u>B</u>eliefs beget Thoughts which beget Feelings which beget <u>B</u>ehavior: <u>B</u>-to-<u>B</u>.

Even though you may intellectually acknowledge that no one person sees everything as it actually occurred, that no one person experiences the same event in the same way, your Concrete Beliefs do not acknowledge these things. They are your *truth*, even if they are not true to others, even if they are irrational. This is why it is so hard to change. This is why we struggle to accept the concrete beliefs of others if they challenge your Concrete Beliefs or worse, threaten your Core Beliefs.

When you think your Core or Concrete Beliefs have been challenged, you typically feel devalued in some way. You may call this *being disrespected* or *offended*. You may feel angry or embarrassed or become defensive. You may even become offensive. These feelings are based in fear and will likely result in a negative reaction. When what you believe is challenged, you become quickly offended because it devalues your life to date. What you have experienced is *truth* and for someone to tell you it is not, seems to diminish you. This is why you may take such challenges so personally. In fact, these feelings should be a warning signal to you; you have just entered the arena of your Core and Concrete Beliefs. If so, you may self-destruct, reacting in anger or withdraw in silence. You may become combative, debating your position with arrogance, intending to minimize the person who challenged you. You might cultivate an *awfulized* perception of a possible outcome if your Concrete, and especially your Core Beliefs are not aligned with the person or event. Your beliefs perpetuate your interpretations and propel your thoughts. Your chosen thoughts create and defend your feelings. Feelings perpetuate your behavior. You think yourself to feel how you believe you should based on what you have experienced in the past or are currently experiencing in the moment. Your beliefs filter your thoughts to shape your perceptions that create your feelings that will predict your behavior.

We are most comfortable when our life, our partner, our friends align with our Concrete and Core Beliefs. Our manifested perception of any of these is the outcome of your thoughts born from your beliefs. If your perception aligns with your beliefs you more than likely will find yourself *attracted* to them or some other notion such as an advertisement, video, song, or even a friendship and relationship. These choices perpetuate beliefs that agree with our current modus operandi and may or may not be rational. So, if it is change you want, you must acknowledge, understand and test your Concrete Beliefs and extract and reframe your Core beliefs. This is very uncomfortable but only by beginning with beliefs, can you get through the thoughts and feelings that lead to behavior. If you want to change a behavior, change your feelings. But to change your feelings you need to change your thoughts; change *what* you think. To change *how* you think, you need to examine and be willing and humble to change what you believe.

You can choose to live in a reality of optimistic hope or cynical fear. You can ride the not so fun pessimistic reality to the outcome or you can choose to ride the optimistic hope to the outcome. If the outcome is not the most desired, at least the ride there was fun. I suggest enjoying the ride in optimistic hope because life isn't about outcome.

I will use a past client to help illustrate the Core Beliefs and the Belief-to-Behavior or B-to-B Principles of Change.

Mary was depressed and having thoughts of suicide. Five years earlier, she divorced her husband for cheating; this was the third time she had caught him. The divorce was followed by two serious relationships in which both men were unfaithful. Mary was now single again and missing work to stay home, sleep and cry. She was sleeping for up to 15 hours a day but awake most of the night. She was hardly eating and rarely showering.

These changes in Mary were striking. She was a successful self-employed businesswoman. In some of our sessions, I noticed just before Mary would break down and cry, she would make the same statements: *Every man is a lying dog. I will always be alone, so I'll never be happy.* Like clockwork, she would return to these sentences in some form just before the tears would flow again. Rather than seek to reassure her, one day I let her vent. I wanted to observe her chosen dialogue and because sometimes people just need to get it out. I call it purging. After about two or three minutes, I asked her, *Would you date every man in the world to find love?* She thought seriously about this question. She eventually replied with a meek and unsure *No?* I followed by asking, *Why then would you include every man in the world in your present definition of men and not in your chances of finding love?* Puzzled, she stared at me. I quickly asked her, *How has having just three or four relationships given you the ability to deem every male on the planet a lying dog?* I quickly changed course by asking her about plans with her best friend. In her venting, she mentioned she had a girls' weekend planned. Mary quickly perked up and eventually rattled off some details. I cut her short and said, *See, you won't even be alone this weekend!* She caught on to me quickly. Mary said, *So I guess I'll actually be happy this weekend, too.* And she smiled when she said it. *You said it*, I replied. She gathered herself, stood up and confidently stated a newly designed belief. Not just a thought. *You know Adam, I did say that! Sure, not all men are dogs, and one day I will meet the right man. Right now I need solitude and some good friends and I am happy!* My eyes watered with joy in her new perspective, her new belief, not just that I knew she would persevere once again, but that she would also be stronger.

With a few fairly obvious questions, Mary assessed her thoughts and statements more rationally, changed her self-dialogue, and provoked an immediate change in her present feelings. She chose to create a more rewarding belief by mastering her chosen dialogue. Mary's new powerful and positive belief was constructed in less than a minute and this reframed her present emotional state. It changed her immediate behavior. Rational dialogue made her emotions more manageable in the moment. She did this by analyzing herself rationally and questioning her concrete beliefs while thinking and speaking more rationally and optimistically to herself about her future. This created a more optimistic present-life narrative. She did this. Not me.

Mary concretely believed she was supposed to feel sadness and loneliness because a relationship had ended. Our society has done a great job showing this to be a negative thing. To quote writer and comedian Lewis C.K. *No good marriage has ended in divorce.* She was increasing the negative emotional potency of this predictable life experience by saying *all men, always alone,* and *never happy*, choosing negative and irrational dialogue to make the present feelings more awful while also reinforcing how she believed she should feel because another relationship had ended because of infidelity. Dr. Albert Ellis calls this *awfulizing*. It might not be a stretch to imagine that Mary's negative concrete beliefs led her to men with negative beliefs about women. We might also see how an independent, joyous and energetic Mary might attract a different partner than a cynical, needy and sad Mary might.

Learn not to pay attention to your initial feelings but more to the thoughts that are creating your feelings and, more importantly, whether those thoughts are rational. A feeling begins with a thought. Your thoughts create your feelings. These feelings drive your behavior. Your behavior and the outcomes typically reinforce the concrete beliefs that led you to those thoughts and feelings, all of which, unchallenged, ultimately writes the narrative of your life.

Your earliest life victories, positive and negative helped reinforced your Core (what you believe about the world, others and self) and your other Concrete Beliefs. In challenging times, you call upon your beliefs many times with seemingly unconscious application of thought. You may feel as if you are just reacting or responding and your feelings are the proof it must be true. Feelings and believing them immediately and behaving on them makes feelings a dangerous word. You create feelings with your thoughts. Feelings you believe to be true because you have or are presently experiencing the roller coaster with your chosen perception. Perhaps enforcing your perception must be true! Dr. Ellis called this *muster*bation: *I must be right. They must be wrong. You must be successful. You must, must, must, must and must.*

You have instinctually and evolutionarily been given the capacity to quickly sort moments and events in life and compare them to a memory of experiences. Your life used to depend on it. Through all your available human senses you download environmental information during multiple life happenings. This data is filter in less than a second through your past experiences looking for references of safe and unsafe, identifiable or a challenge. Meanwhile you are judging the event on your personal set of values and beliefs or what you have accepted to be true or right, threatening or nonthreatening to your safety and values. Once you have found a reference experience it combines with your present beliefs regarding the environment and event. This produces your thoughts, thoughts you meticulously organize to create your feelings related to your past experiences, environments, and present event enforcers. You then act based on the given interpretation and created feelings. If the environment or event does not match your beliefs, you more than likely will become defensive or even offensive.

Imagine you lived in the time before man made safe and secure structures and lived in mass numbers. You and some of your group were sitting around a fire at night. You hear some brush break and suddenly a large shadow of a monster zips through camp and takes a member of your group. Perhaps this caused you to run, hide or fight at that very moment. Perhaps at the next fire you will form a tighter group and be ready to defend yourself, maybe even set traps. I'll bet at the next fire sitting you will be ready to react defensively when you hear the brush break. This is how your life came to depend on this ability. It still does. It is just not a saber-tooth tiger. In this time, it is more about avoiding attacks from suppose to's, social constructs and being eaten by social, mental and physical illnesses.

Remember that your chosen thoughts create your feelings. You react to feelings because you believe your thoughts to be fact. After all, they are rooted in your personal experience and life values so they feel as though they must be true. Some call this instinct, intuition or even survival. I mean hey, when the brush breaks, you better be ready, right? But it could also be your friend from the other group stopping by to say hello. Do not end up rationalizing and intellectualizing yourself to be right, to prove your initial feelings to be fact just because you have experienced something similar. To be the only allowed fact or perception is irrational. Yes, all of this happens in a second or so. You are an amazing creature, aren't you? Agreed. These words lack the true power of the human species, the power to control thoughts regardless of environmental influence or primal instinct. To reason, think, contemplate and plan.

> *To face the wolf in the winter cold, you will need to be steady with your thoughts, with your fears, and with your spear.*
> -300 (THE MOVIE)

You have the power of reason and thought control. You become the maestro of your emotions by becoming the master of your thoughts. You become the master of your thoughts by weighing and measuring your chosen beliefs. You choose the notes that move you.

You are what you repeatedly believe, think and choose to do daily. If it is feelings and behavior you want to change, then we know that you need to first change what you believe and think. This is how you break the cycle of stagnation and even regression.

Your thoughts create your feelings. Have I driven this point home enough? Let's do a quick experiment. You are an actor sitting for an audition. This audition requires you to perform intense and wide-ranging emotions in a moment. Are you ready? Here we go. First, I want you to feel sorrow right now. Show me sorrow. What are you thinking? Now, quickly, show me joy. I want you to feel joy. What are you thinking? You see, you had to create a thought from a past experience or a belief to produce the thoughts that conjured the emotions. You control your emotions, not *them*, *they*, *it* or the past. You are in charge of your feelings.

Your thoughts are yours alone. You choose to believe them or question them. But to openly and honestly question them, you need to practice humility. You may have normalized your behavior and proudly announce *It is just who I am!* when you face a threat to your beliefs. More likely, this is your defense when you know you are wrong but have no idea why or how to change it. Like a self-accepting broken machine of insanity, you repeat life methods expecting different results, wondering why you can't change. But what would happen if you stopped declaring that you cannot change, stopped blaming the world and others and seized the opportunity to experience life and growth? Perhaps you have participated in or experienced too many traumatic experiences to list. Maybe violence is all that has been modeled for you. Or perhaps you were just ignored; made to feel unworthy and unimportant. Maybe life has just been hard; nothing was easy, it was one punch of pain after another. Remember, B-You.

Your life experiences created the cement that molded your Core and Concrete Beliefs. Your personal perception is intellectualized and rationalized as a *must-be-true*. This allows the irrational thought *It is just who I am*. This statement repeated solidifies the present chosen life narrative and truly is a passive acceptance and a concrete statement of surrender. It allows no room for growth. But if you can reframe your life experiences, might there be different beliefs created? More specifically, modify present perceptions by reframing negative concrete beliefs and thoughts to be more positive and include rational dialogue. Well, you can! This creates an immediate change in present feelings, if you get out of your own way. If your current beliefs are perpetuating thoughts, feelings and behaviors you want to change, then you need to change those beliefs. You are on a mission to cultivate, reveal, and reframe your negative and irrational Core and Concrete Beliefs. You will need to dig into your internal dialogue, beneath your surface beliefs, to reveal your Core Beliefs.

You may discover that your Core and even some Concrete Beliefs, although negative or irrational protected you, worked for you in the most trying of times or your early life victories, as I referred to them. To question any of your Core or Concrete Beliefs related to these moments may feel as though you are devaluing your entire life to date. But what you needed then, what protected you then, may be paralyzing you today. This is what it feels like to question your Concrete and Core Beliefs. Real change is not just saying different words. This is not just wordplay. This is why you have more than likely avoided it at all costs. It can be uncomfortable, but...

Uncomfortable is where the change is.

To be clear, your *Core Beliefs, what you believe about the world, others and self* are concreted currently. Whether they are negative, positive, rational or irrational will soon be discovered and discerned by you. Any other belief that you unwaveringly perceive to be truth is a Concrete Belief. If your Core Beliefs (all your other beliefs foundations) are negative and irrational, you will remain weighed down and you will continue to drown. To defend these beliefs many times you may begin to count on your hands all the reasons you have for thinking, feeling and behaving as you do. You are dispersing blame with statements you believe to be fact. This is you building a case with your thoughts to confirm your feelings and rationalize yourself right. I know, these experiences sure feel real at the time. Pause. Remember the roller-coaster perspective. You may miss what you immediately think. You are simply trained to feel for what you think. Emotions stated as fact are only based in past experiences and present perceptions, perceptions that you have concreted *Manchurian* like responses over your lifetime.

I cannot stress enough that before you can change you have to be aware of your Core and Concrete Beliefs. You need to be willing to first accept that negative beliefs are perceptions and are able to be replaced with more rational positive perceptions. You have to learn to become *the master of the silver lining* to master a life change. Remember, truth is formed in the plasticity of belief. Your beliefs create thoughts. Thoughts cultivate feelings, and feelings perpetuate your behavior. There is a silver lining, so hunt for it. Hunt for it as hard as you fought to declare your negative beliefs to be fact.

If the beliefs you currently hold have gotten you here, why hold on to them with such vigor? Which beliefs are promoting positive thoughts, and which are holding you in negative concrete boots? I know it sounds like wordplay, but just challenging your Core and Concrete Beliefs can be one of the most difficult mental tasks, especially if you perceive it to be. Soon you will begin to constructed new positive, but rational concrete beliefs that will be reinforced through your self-talk and behavior choices. Over time this creates real and lasting changes. Learning to recognize, observe, analyze and reframe your self-talk reduces redlining feelings and poor behavioral responses.

Remember *Core Beliefs: What you believe about the world, others and self* are your foundation upon which all your other Concrete Beliefs are built. You choose the dialogue. You create the perception. You define your belief.

> *Feelings aren't facts, and just because you think it, it doesn't make it so.*
> -LEO D'ANIIBALLE

CHAPTER 6

THE H=C PRINCIPLE

Those who seek knowledge must begin with humbleness.
—Buju Banton

Before you can change or even discover your negative concrete beliefs, you must begin from a place of humility. Not just an awareness, but a consistent, relentless practice of humility. Acknowledge and accept, that you don't know anything for certain. You can believe that. Humility, openness and self-awareness are where change begins and this mindset needs continue throughout your life. In fact, if you are feeling stuck or discouraged, check your humility mindset first. Somewhere along your journey, did you decide you know enough, have learned enough, have changed enough and now you are the master of beliefs?

Humility is defined in many ways. I am not a fan of the *Oxford Dictionary* definition. The truth is you will constantly define it as you cultivate it. To me, humility is not thinking less of yourself, but thinking more of others. It is allowing that you may not really understand or appreciate someone else's concrete beliefs, their truth. Or perhaps you understand their beliefs but they are not true for you; perhaps they are even reprehensible to you. Humility avoids judgment; instead, humility seeks to give grace. It is a practice, not something you are or become. To call oneself humble is hypocritical in its very essence. To me, humility is not powerless or passive. It is powerful, stoic and influential because it is tolerant in response to self, others and the world. It is transparent and strong. Those attitudes attract people, thoughts and ideas rather than attack or ridicule them.

Practicing humility empowers you to pause when the urgency of life rampages upon you. Pause to analyze your thoughts before allowing your feelings to fully engage. It allows time to see wisdom in the fearful moments of life. It is not fear or weakness; it is a choice you make when others choose anger or scorn or ridicule. Even when wronged, humility does require silence or acceptance. It is a humble pronouncement of your truth.

Humility is not only a Principle of Change; it is a jackhammer to the negative concrete beliefs that are weighing you down. With a humble attitude, you discover your negative concrete beliefs. Only through humility are you going to be able to reconstruct those negative beliefs with a more rational and optimistic framework.

A linear life is created with a concrete mind, a never-ending line to the same people, places, and things, a line to the same outcome. Through humility, you can learn to eventually enjoy the multiple perceptions of yourself and others, endless angles on situations, on people, on truth. You will not accept them all as your truth today, but the knowledge will change your perspective. Criticism (constructive or otherwise) is your friend from now on. It provides a glimpse into what others are seeing in you and your world. It is not necessarily accurate or true but it may be an honest perception of you that they created. These perceptions, true or not, prevent us from connecting with others; they are something we must all be willing to see and to change, revealing our true self and not the image others have of us.

Mistakes now become your master teachers; we learn more from our mistakes than our successes if we are humble enough to acknowledge and exam them. Once closely examined with a humble Spirit, we may realize the mistake we made was not at all the obvious misstep but rather an error in judgment, an assumption we made or an attitude that we projected. As my mentor Leo D'Anniballe would say, *Never miss the opportunity to say nothing*. This is true of criticism; criticism can teach you about you. But I would like to add *and learn something*. This in truth is the point of all humility. Humility opens the door to learning, learning about ourselves, about family, about others and about the world. And learning brings knowledge and understanding; a concept I call Competence. Humility is powerful and propels you to meaningful learning. Through humility, you find authentic Competence. This is the H=C Principle of Change; Humility produces Competence. Self competence.

CHAPTER 7

THE CCE PRINCIPLE

There is a difference between an authentic
confidence and a false confidence.

Humility is the first step to change, to growth and to self-competence. One of the competencies you may acquire through humility is learned empathy; this is empathy that comes from accepting and understanding that those that harmed you are handicapped by their own negative concrete beliefs. Learned empathy does not require you to understand or pity your harmers. The only way I have found to move beyond those who have hurt you terribly is to learn empathy in order to become authentically indifferent. Only then can you move forward. Forgiveness to me is not necessary. This is a spiritual contender. You can move forward in life without forgiveness, past the trauma, all of it. But learned empathy is the only door to true apathy I have discovered.

Another competency that humility will lead you to is acceptance that there are no *supposed to's* in life. If I asked you *Is life fair?* how would you respond? If you believe life is supposed to be fair, this a good place to start. Examine this negative and irrational concrete belief. Life is not supposed to be anything, including fair. Life includes people and with people, even family and friends, there is no *normal* pre-determined way. There are standards, expectations, there are preferences, even role models (good and bad). These either help or hinder our relationships. But there is no universally-agreed upon set of *supposed to's*. To quote Doc

Holliday in the movie *Tombstone, There is no normal life, Wyatt. There's just life.*

The H=C Principle, in daily practice, brings more insights, more awareness of self and others, more rational beliefs, more competencies. This lays the path to an authentic self-confidence. Self-awareness leads to self-competence, which leads to an authentic self-confidence. This is not a self-confidence built on arrogance, judgment and irrational beliefs. This is a self-confidence that is at once humble and eager. You are confident because you know what you don't know but are enthusiastically in search of it. It is not just excitement; it is an unwavering enthusiasm for your life. Be careful not to tip the balance of humility and authentic self-confidence. Continue the pursuit toward self-awareness and self-confidence by daily practicing humility.

A consistent and humbled search for self-competence begins you toward enthusiasm, not Zen. Think about something you are enthusiastic in doing. How do you feel when you are performing this activity? Happy I hope. But how did you get confident performing this activity or confident the activity would produce happiness or flow? You got competent is what, why, and how. You sought out competence and this created experiences that gave you confidence over time, and if continued can produce happiness. This cultivated a path to a state of happiness for you, by you. A path created by using your perceptions of an event or life experience. This is why you are enthusiastic about practices, events, moments and situations you are confident will reward you. This can apply to negative activities as well because they, too, produce rewards of enthusiastic states.

The CCE Principle of Change states that Competence creates Confidence and Confidence creates Enthusiasm. The cultivated enthusiasm is a state of happiness built on an authentic confidence. A false confidence is merely based on words or declarations made internally or externally and is not founded on genuine competence or experience, but on creating a perception of competence. In fact, false confidence is often overcompensation for fear and insecurity; it can easily be pierced.

Seeking competence is an experience unto itself. It can be sought and found in many ways: intentional self-reflection, seeking and receiving criticism and evaluation from others, purposeful reading and research. But the experience of seeking competence is often the teacher. Sometimes, when all the plans and strategies for seeking competencies fail, the most unintended or accidental experiences can provide a breakthrough.

My point is that nearly each breath in and out is an experience producing competence if you are listening, seeking and observing the world, others and self, not judging and expecting. Experiences also simply happens to you. It is what your today and yesterday gave you. Understand that each life experience, each minute can give you competence if you are humble enough to question self, listen, absorb, examine and learn from others. This is how you obtain authentic self-competence, competence based in your truth, not your irrational beliefs, thoughts and feelings.

As stated in the CCE Principle, gaining competence creates confidence and confidence can detonate enthusiasm. Herein lies the state of happiness. It is enthusiasm you are after. True enthusiasm can only be obtained and maintained through your humbled quest for competence, wherever it may be found. Seek self-competence, even if self-observation and personal awareness is your only resource. Cultivate and question what you believe about yourself, others and the world. Question everything and demand evidence; be rational in your search or you may unintentionally build new negative concrete beliefs. Sometimes this search will ignite a hidden passion. Believe me, passion is fleeting. Focusing on creating or spotting the opportunities to challenge your beliefs and gain competencies will create a flow that you can enthusiastically sustain. If you seek to be happy, to be enthusiastic about life, feeding your desire for competencies will get you there, humility and peace will keep you there. Understand there will continuously be things to learn in the world, from others and about self. Make equal time for mental peace; a non seeking mental stillness. Do this as equally as you chase competence and experience. Stillness too is an experience.

These are the powerful Principles of Change and they are based entirely on your beliefs. They are as positive and powerful as you make them.

Side Note Regarding Competence and Anxiety:

Competence, the lack thereof, or even the obsessive chase of also plays a dramatic role in the level of anxiety you feel in a given situation. Many times, when you are in a state of stagnation or transition, it is what is unknown that can be the scariest and, therefore, what you avoid. This does not help you.

The pursuit of competence can lower redlining anxiety and even reduce depression. For example, you wake up in the morning with a growth on your neck the size of a baseball. You freak out, right? Right. Your anxiety is through the roof and your thoughts have you in a panic. You go to the doctor who tells you not to worry. They explain what and why and answer all your questions. They give you some anti-thing cream, tell you to do some healthy things you should be doing anyway and promise you it will be gone for good very soon. Now you are back home, where you were just freaking out. The thing is still on your neck but you are calmer than when you first awoke. The one thing that changed is that you gained knowledge and understanding from a credible source; you gained competence. This helped manage your anxiety.

Questioning your Concrete Beliefs can create anxiety; you are finding tumors, cracks in the foundation. Experiencing a life transition, whether positive or negative, can create anxiety, sometimes to a dangerous level. Gaining knowledge and understanding (competence) with a humble heart and teachable attitude will help ease the anxiety. Humility and competence are wonder drugs with no harmful side-effects.

PHASE III: TOOLS OF CHANGE

CHANGE HOW YOU THINK BY KNOWING WHAT YOU BELIEVE.

CHAPTER 8

RATIONAL SELF-ANALYSIS (RSA)

The unexamined life is not worth living.
—SOCRATES

If you have read this far, you have shown an interest, a willingness to change your life by taking a deeper look at your beliefs. This is both brave and exhilarating. You have decided not to simply accept or resign yourself to *it is what it is*. With an understanding of the Principles of Change, I want to provide you tools to help you apply the principles to an examination of your life, to moments and memories. The Tools of Change you are given here are needed before we move into the Components of Change, the next part of your Cognitive Rampage. The Rational Self-Analysis Tool of Change will help you change the concrete belief of *it is what it is*, to *it is what you make it*.

The RSA Tool of Change helps you unearth and assess negative concrete beliefs that are seeding irrational or negative thoughts, thoughts that consistently stir and reinforce your maladaptive feelings. Those feelings that are perpetuating your unwanted and unhealthy behaviors. RSA will also help you diffuse and cushion the rushing emotions which are inevitable in life's events and experiences. Learning to apply RSA will teach you how to reframe negative concrete beliefs and the thoughts they generate to be more rational. Through rational dialogue reconstruction you will build and use self-talk that is not just positive in thought, but which reflects your Life Philosophy. This is not just wordplay. This is rewiring how you think and process events and information.

Your mind is adaptable and moldable. It is how you have come to believe, think, feel and behave as you do today. You can program and reprogram your thinking process, your beliefs and your life. Keep the Principles of Change ever-present in your mind as you learn to apply RSA. Apply RSA overtime reprograms how you think, not just what you think. Take it slow. Allow you mind to rewire itself. As you write sentences and RSA calls for you to analyze them, stay humble and show yourself grace and patience. Learn to become an observer of your thoughts, a witness to them instead of an instrument of them. Pause instead of react.

Become an observer of your thoughts, not a reactor.

What are the ingredients to a thought? The individual words themselves are the ingredients to a thought. Each powerful word shapes the thought's intention. Remove one word and the thought may change its entire meaning or impact. I suggest the book *Tyranny of Words* by Stuart Chase for a exemplary look into words and language. Words matter. Your intentions behind word choices matter. What are your intentions with the words you choose? The answer to this question needs to be honest, not superficial. Your first answer may be simple and straightforward but is it the whole truth? For example, are you just explaining how you feel or are you intending to prove how you feel to be a fact, that you are right to feel this way?

I want you to think of your favorite recipe. The go-to recipe of yours that everyone loves you to make. Imagine that I have asked you to cook this recipe ten times in a row, but I needed them all to taste exactly the same. How much attention would you need to pay to each ingredient as you weigh and measure it, the order in which you added them, the exact temperature at which each is cooked to make each of your ten dishes taste exactly alike? This task would require extreme focus, observation and attention to detail, of course. The words you choose are the ingredients to the recipe of your thoughts. No longer throw in the first emotional ingredients you feel to make or continue to make your irrational recipe of thought. Pay close and cautious attention to your internal dialogue. Words hold meaning and power. Words shape intention and amplify tone. Words form pictures in your mind. Irrational words form irrational thoughts that paint pictures of impossibility. How you talk to yourself matters.

Our words, our self-talk typically reflects our Core and other Concrete Beliefs which probably formed long ago; you may not even be aware of the basis for them. But these judgmental beliefs are reinforced constantly by our culture. We have been taught to judge quickly and instantly, without much analysis or thought. With its *like* buttons, star ratings, personal reviews, followers, and internet matchmaking, it is quick and easy to destroy a product or promote a phony cause. We are continually told our opinion matters. We are empowered to be judgmental, encouraged to be critical. Companies regularly ask us to post our ratings, complete a survey, provide feedback, as though our opinion is so important they might change the way they do business if we give them a bad review. But is any of that true?

This culture may have trained you to become a professional customer and critic. Cultures all over the world seem to be quickly injecting this ideal in all its potency. Yes, this technology gives us access to all the world's competence, happenings and opinions. It has connected the world, toppled evil regimes and informs a global community—greatest strength, greatest weakness. It is not surprising then that in a society of constant and instant criticism, we are relentless critics of ourselves and others. Add to this harmful condition, the psychological manipulation of your self-image by advertisers and our concrete beliefs in absurd social constructs become crippling. In a sense, you may have become a subservient self-important martyr who sees no need for self-reflection. Your personal perceptions are the only truth allowed. You behave as though life will read your Trip Advisor review and make adjustments accordingly. You may have become concrete in your *supposed to's* while accusing the world and others of doing the same. It is these self-inflicted daily judgments soaked in assumptions and expectations that are most destructive to your inner narrative, your life's story, others and the world.

There is a difference between self-criticism and self-analysis

When you are in a state of stagnation, pain or transition, you tend to become the master of self-criticism. You stop using your human capabilities of observation, analysis and reason. You may become overly critical of yourself believing this will somehow motivate you, when in turn it will eventually lead to self-pity or despair. You will believe it to be so overtime. Or you may become judgmental of your environment, friends, family, any one or any thing, blaming them for the state of your life. You may become sensitive, taking offense at any perceived criticism from others. You may choose to isolate yourself or gather people around you who make you feel better about yourself because they are in a worse place than you. You are already lashing out at yourself so you cannot even begin to see opposing views as opportunities for growth. You feel like you are on your last bit of *fake it till you make it,* all you have left before you start killing ants with shotguns. To be wrong about anything in a transition state feels devastating, and many times as if it is a threat to who you are as a person. You defend, run or push at the first feeling of conflict. Who wouldn't want to numb this out? You make defensive and declarative statements of perceived fact to paint the picture you think you *should* paint because you feel it to be true. You keep your wounds *feeling* fresh with your meticulously chosen thoughts, behaviors and environments. Trust me, you know what you are doing.

Perhaps these feelings are familiar to you because you have experienced similar wounds in the past. Your past experiences must be the right perception of this experience. Who said you must feel a particular way because a particular event happened? Why must you react in a certain way? This is what *musterbating* sounds like. *I must be rich. I must be in a relationship. I must be happy. I must be successful. I must react this way. I must be right. I must be sad when a relationship ends. People and the world must treat me fairly.* You may be using responses and strategies that worked for you in the past or gave you an early life victory or two. This includes defense mechanisms or coping skills you concretely believe helped you survive and or obtain a life victory such as overcoming an abusive relationship, sudden loss or childhood neglect, abandonment or abuse. Your early life victories helped concrete your present-day Core and Concrete Beliefs, responses to people, places and events, as well as shape your coping skills and present life narrative. The problem is these beliefs and coping skills may not have been healthy then or may no longer work or apply in your present. They were the go-to beliefs and methods in monumental moments of your past. Even if they didn't really work then, perhaps you believed the outcome is what you deserved. These beliefs, strategies and responses may not be positively rewarding you any longer as they once did and you are forcing squares in circles. I mean, they worked once before during the crucial moments and pivotal times in your life, so they *must* work now! And if they don't, *it's you not me!* Others and the world are to blame if they do not provide a victory. You will continue to use these strategies despite their outcomes because it is what you have experienced to work. Negative rewards often times can also become repeated rewards we create for ourselves. Self-punishment many times is even a reward because you believe you deserve it. But this is simply playing the martyr and it is still self-serving.

Your past experiences and early life victories have shaped your beliefs and responses to events. You may have even built your present environment or lifestyle to be similar to the one you resent. You do this because you are comfortable in it, even if you know and others see its negative impact. Your beliefs and behaviors work in this type of environment despite you knowing the environment's destructive nature. Since you work in this environment, it, and especially you, cannot be wrong. Others and/or the world must be screwed up. This becomes the normalizing dialogue: you-against-the-world life narrative, a belief that may have helped you to normalize abuse, negativity, loss, and perceived failure. This was first done by you to survive the past and give you your first early life victories. It is what you know how to do. This is what rewards you. It is who you believe yourself to be or even what you believe yourself to deserve.

Emotions are learned, then practiced.

Your early life victories may have gone unnoticed to you in their very specifics, but you've had them. You use the coping skills you currently do because they produced a victory or victories (rewards) at the most trying times in your life. Those early victories shaped your current responses, coping skills, current life narrative, emotional reactions, and choices. You are a species of trial and error. Using what works repeatedly for rewards. This is especially true in times of perceived fear or hurt. You tend to go to the quickest, least self-reflective routes and stick to the more comfortable and known paths and responses, even if they are self-destructive. These paths also produce intellectualizations you use to prove yourself to be right time and time again. Being right begins to become more important than being aware. You may even deem these intellectualizations as constructive even though they require the least amount of effort and analysis. They help you avoid the possibility that it may be personal ignorance. You deconstruct the event, others, and the world to be wrong rather than yourself because that *feels* better. It is easier, and not to mention one more time being wrong may be the last mental straw before those ants are done for!

Most of what you say in periods of stagnation or transition ends with a period or an exclamation point. Your truth may feel like it is the only thing keeping you alive or keeping you *normal* so you cannot question it. You do not question it. You do not criticize it. But there is an important difference between self-criticism and self-analysis. Self-criticism comes in statements of truth as you perceive it. Self-analysis comes in the form of questions seeking understanding of one's own feelings, thoughts, beliefs and perceptions. Learn to become an observer of your thoughts, not a reactor. Be aware of which thoughts are creating your feelings. Learn to question your initial feelings by searching the thoughts creating them, and especially the beliefs that seed those thoughts.

I will continue to remind you to learn to become the master of the silver lining. Believe many problems are rare opportunities. Many lean toward talking about and focusing on their problem perception. Some make emotional statements of perceived fact to reinforce initial feelings. If they are not making subjecting statements, the most frequently asked questions begin *How could they? How did this happen? Who is responsible for this happening to me?* When a problem occurs, rather than hunt for blame and fault, question your thoughts that are creating your current feelings. You have been given the power of self-reflection and reason, the ability to take feedback as reward, the ability to change dialogue to change perception to change immediate feelings. Hunt for the silver lining as hard as you hunted to be right in the past. This mission you have begun will require a new special set of skills. I've always wanted to say that. You will need new skills, strategies, thinking processes, behaviors and especially beliefs.

Remember how Mary awfulized her situation with her chosen dialogue and peppered it with unlikely or even impossibilities? *Every man is a lying dog. I will always be alone, so I will never be happy. Awfulizing situations*, using negative language that is exaggerated is an example of irrational thinking. Mary was choosing dialogue that created her recipe of perpetual negative thinking fueled by her negative and irrational beliefs. This thought process proves her rushing emotions and feelings to be right because she believes them to be. It is a poor attempt to express feelings of hurt and fear, unknowingly perpetuating sadness, self-doubt and fear.

Thinking is defined as the process of using one's mind to consider or reason about something. Mary was not thinking, analyzing or considering. She was declaring her feelings as though they were fact. I define irrational thinking: *a thinking process about a subjective idea that is based in a negative perception resulting in negative thoughts, reinforced by negative dialogue to support and enhance the probability of a bad or awful outcome.* RSA helps you identify irrational thinking and thoughts, alerts and guides you to the negative and many time concrete beliefs seeding the irrational thoughts or thinking pattern. Again, learn to become an observer of your thoughts, not a reactor, and find the silver lining.

Applying Rational Self-Analysis (RSA):

I have spent some time describing and giving you examples of irrational thinking. Rather than explain the theory of rational thinking, I have provided a tool to help you retrain your mind to begin to think more rationally. Your first Tool of Change, Rational Self-Analysis, or RSA, will help you reframe your thinking pattern over time, filter irrational thoughts and reduce negatively charged emotional reactions while also revealing your deeply entwined Core Beliefs (what you have accepted to be true about yourself, others and the world) as well as negative concrete beliefs that are producing your irrational thoughts that are perpetuating your destructive feelings that are perpetuating your unwanted behavior. These are the beliefs you are seeking to change, the Negative Core and Concrete Beliefs, the root of your irrational thinking, if you will. For this, you will need to build a garrison for your mind. A *garrison* is a force of protection, a stronghold, often the first line of defense placed in front of the fort with orders to defend against anything that comes within sight unless ordered to stand down. The RSA Tool of Change is your mental garrison, set in place to target negative concrete beliefs and protect you from irrational thought infiltration. This tool will help you navigate the belief canvas of your mind.

Use the RSA Tool of Change to freeze a moment or event in life when the emotions hurtling at you are creating a sense of urgency or defense that may be untrue or unnecessary. Pause; that is just fear creating the urgency. It's not real unless you perceive it to be (or there really is a lion coming after you). Do not just react to your body, your feelings or thoughts.

> *Feelings are not facts, and just because you think it, it doesn't make is so.*
> LEO D'ANNIBALLE

Applying the RSA Tool of Change in a moment in life or to analyze one of the Components of Change both begin the same way. Pause to analyze and observe your thoughts. Pause to prevent reacting to your initial emotions steaming from your thoughts of self-created urgency and or fear. Pause to analyze your initial feelings thoroughly by investigating your initial inner or outer dialogue. Your thoughts are creating your feelings. Do not react to the rushing feelings; move past them to the thoughts that came first. Remember, feelings aren't facts, and you do not have to run or push away. Many times, you do not *have* to do anything at all. Pause and observe the punctuation and tone of your internal narrative. Statements end with periods and exclamation points, as if they are facts. This leaves no room for the plasticity of your perceptions to work positively for you. Analysis is done with questions and humility. It is not done with statements. Criticism is done with subjective statements declared as fact. There is no humility being practiced in making subjective statements of perceived truth to defend emotions. Challenge your internal or external statement by changing the punctuation to a question mark. Make your statement a question and you may reveal something about yourself. If the revelation still eludes you, refer to the wonderful curiosity of children and simply ask yourself *why* questions over and over: *Why do I believe what I believe? Why am I allowing these thoughts if they are creating these feelings? Why am I responding as though my feelings are fact?* You serve yourself better to ask, *Why does this person's behavior challenge my beliefs and does it actually affect me? Why am I treating this like a top five in life? Why am I allowing this to flow through me and not around me?* Defensive, subjective statements of your perception are no longer your first reaction. It is what has actually been holding you back from growth. You chose the dialogue and chose to believe it. Self-directed *why* questions spoken in a curious humble tone create opportunities for self-analysis and work better than drawing lines in the sand.

To help you recognize irrational beliefs and thoughts, I will arm you with the awareness of words I call *determinant words*. An appearance by one of these words is a big red flag that what you just thought or said is most likely irrational. Determinant words are exaggerations of the past, present and future. They linguistically predetermine and can awfulize the past, present and future. I like to say that these determinant words (and phrases), are the only real curse words: *try, always, never, should(n't), would(n't), could(n't), can't, must, have to, had to, supposed to, all the time, everyone, everywhere, assume,* and *expected.* Notice next time how your body almost does not even want to say these words. You almost have to push the word out as you elongate the pronunciation. For example, *You alllways do this to me! It is neeever going to change,* or *Eeeveryone thinks...* Listen to your thoughts and observe your body. It will tell you much of what is happening in the present with your mind, so observe it as well. Do not just react to it. If you are wildly pacing, breathing and speaking, this is a reflection of your present mind. More than likely there is not a lion trying to eat you. Slow down, and remember to pause first. Observe your thoughts for negative tone, statement punctuation and determinant words.

Determinant words assume the future and rule out hope, chance, and change—*crystal-ball thinking*, I like to call it. They are an attempt to pre-determine an outcome before action and many times are used to awfulize or exaggerate the potential outcome. They infect your life's narrative. They often make others immediately defensive because you have now included them in your negative belief. They concrete negative percep-tions into awfulized negative beliefs. Remember Mary and her irrational statements? *Every man is a lying dog, I will always be alone, so I'll never be happy.* How many red flags did you see? All statements essentially end with a period. Each statement consists of a determinant word, as well. Contrary to some people's beliefs, *every* man is not a lying dog. Obviously, she was not going to *always* be alone. Last, can people be happy alone? Of course they can. Mary and I discovered after some time applying RSA together that her negative concrete belief was, *I can't be happy alone.* This was her deep-seated negative concrete belief perpetuating the present irrational thoughts. Identifying her irrational thoughts eventually led her to reveal this negative concrete belief, a belief that has been perpetuating her sad and hopeless feelings. This negative concrete belief also affected Mary's choice of partner, many times forcing relationships from urgency, ignoring red flags that were flying from day one. With a negative con-crete belief, turned negative Core Belief of, *I can't be happy alone* running her thinking, choices and behavior, it is no wonder why Mary is taking her failed relationships so hard. With this negative belief at her core, her happiness depends on others.

Mary's reframed thought, *Right now I need solitude and some good friends and I am happy.* created a very quick positive emotional response and holds an optimistic tone. Mary reframed her irrational dialogue to create a more rational and optimistic thought. If she allows this newly reframed and rational thought to flow through her or become her automatic thought, it will manifest into her feelings and behavior over time. The rewards of feelings and behaviors in her new experiences will eventually solidify new positive concrete beliefs. Using rational dialogue controls the emotional onslaught. This is exactly how *I can't be happy alone* became a part of her Core Belief about self. A negative concrete Core Belief. We simply installed new positive and rational beliefs by analyzing the irrationality of her negative thoughts and beliefs.

RSA is how you begin to retrain yourself to analyze and not simply react. You can use RSA on any thought, feeling, event or concrete belief. You will apply RSA to each Component of Change. Think of applying RSA to these Components of Change as a treatment to retrain how you think. You are rewiring your brain functioning to help you begin to observe and not react to your feelings and thoughts, help you learn to pause to observe your initial thoughts, to look for the thoughts that are creating your initial emotions. You may have to dig deep to reveal your Core and Concrete Beliefs. Do not expect this to just come naturally. You are reprogramming your entire life's thinking process.

Practice, practice, practice. Observe your daily inner and outer dialogue for determinant words. Check yourself for negative pessimistic phrases and feelings. Practice reframing your irrational dialogue as often as you can. Practice with events and actions not emotionally charged, events that entail less emotion. If you hear yourself use a determinant word, repeat the thought or sentence again without using the determinant word. Practice not using determinant words even in your everyday speech, especially when thinking to yourself. Observe for negative tone that harbors a pessimistic narrative. Reframe your sentence if you discover a determinant word or if it holds a negative tone, pessimistic outlook or irrational implications. Make your dialogue an observation experiment. RSA will help you learn to observe your inner dialogue and challenge and change your perceptions. You will begin to reframe your life by first reframing your internal dialogue. This will curb feelings toward old and new experiences that will concrete new positive but rational beliefs. You will truly begin to be the writer of your life narrative, not *it*, *them*, *they* or the past.

You have continued to use the same dialogue to reinforce your Core Beliefs about yourself, others, and the world based on your perception of past and current life experiences. It seems only rational to install new beliefs the same way the current ones got there. You will need to clear the deeply rooted negative Core and Concrete Beliefs before you can begin to pour new ones. Using RSA, you will reveal your negative concrete beliefs (if you have them) as you work at each Component of Change. Each time you apply RSA, remember to keep the Principles of Change in mind. You will apply RSA for identifying irrational thoughts and revealing negative concrete beliefs in need of reframing as they pertain to each specific Component to Change. Again, Dr. Albert Ellis, in my opinion, is the one to read if you want more knowledge (competency) regarding irrational thinking.

You and I will work RSA together directly on the Components of Change, but here is the step-by-step application of RSA. Don't worry I will expand on the dialogue in future chapters, but it is the five-step process of applying RSA that is important to remember here. (1) Pause and ask yourself what you believe about the given Component, event, person or situation. (2) Write your answer down beginning with the words *I believe*. (3) Begin the RSA Q&A's for analysis by simply asking *Why?* to each reply. *Why do I believe*, etc. This will produce another statement. Write it down and ask *why* to this statement. Continue the Q&As while closely observing your dialogue, tone, and narrative. Write down your *I believe* answer and ask why to each response until you think you have revealed one or more concrete beliefs. Ask *why* until you annoy yourself. Your frustration will reveal your typical emotionally verbal reaction. Observe and listen for determinant words. These are red flags to inform you that what you said or thought is irrational. It may even be the negative concrete belief you are hunting. Tracking the dialogue that is creating your feelings will lead you down the path toward revealing your negative concrete belief if you have one. More than likely, it is tied to that intellectualized statement you keep repeating as your answer to reinforce your initial concrete belief. Hunt humbly.

Once you believe you have revealed your negative concrete belief through the RSA Q&As, irrational thought and determinant word identification and you have written it all down, move to Step (4) Reframe your discovered negative and irrational belief. In your reframing of this thought be sure not to use determinant words, and frame your new thought to be positive but rational, and attempt to end your new thought to be optimistic in measure. Your newly reframed thought is called your Belief Sentence. Construct each Belief Sentence by beginning with the word *Remember*. Shape your sentence as though you are leaving instructions or advice for yourself. You know you give great advice. After you have reframed (reconstructed) your new rational and positive Belief Sentence (5) add this new Belief Sentence to your Life Philosophy or LP. You will soon construct a Belief Sentence for every Component of Change by applying RSA to each. Once you have done so you will have cultivated your *Life Philosophy Foundation*.

Mary reframed well for her first attempt, *Not every man is a dog, and one day I will meet the right man. Right now I need solitude and some good friends and I am happy.* This too could be analyzed for irrationalities, but it is a dramatic improvement from her initial beliefs that were perpetuating her sadness. Simply reframing thoughts with new words is word play. Extracting and being willing to change concrete beliefs is a much deeper level leaving lasting change. I suggest you begin by writing down all you cultivate and discover. Eventually you will be able to perform RSA aloud or in your mind. Practice, practice, practice. You are now in mental training! Your thoughts, feelings, and behaviors have now become your research project. Observe. Observe. Analyze. Analyze. Reframe—your beliefs and thoughts. This is the only thing you truly control.

Your irrational thoughts and determinant words are the beacons to your negative concrete beliefs that need to be reframed. Repeat the RSA process as needed to any component, concrete belief or event that comes to your mind or life. RSA will also reveal to you where you need to seek competence and change. It will also reveal to you new interests. This will begin to happen when you are working your I-to-E Inventory with RSA and your LP Foundation together in the last chapters. Continue to analyze even your newly constructed Belief Sentences. Remain humble in your discoveries. Be careful what you concrete, if anything.

Utilize your cognitive flexibility.
-Dr. Carl Hart

You have thought yourself to feel this way and allowed it to manifest to truth. Remember, *Don't should all over yourself*, as Leo and I like to say. Remember, your feelings come from an instinctive reaction of survival gained from past experiences of personal life victories used to protect your truth. There is no truth, only perceived reality in this physical and conscious world to which we currently live. Remember, others have a right to their perception and beliefs just as you do, and you do not get to determine whether you think you are being an asshole. Belief principles: if you are to expand your mind and grow, then you will need to be willing to be wrong, and that is OK. H=C Principle. Rational Self-Analysis helps you explore yourself and grow from others' perceptions and experiences with the world. This opens you up for change and feeds competence. CCE principle. No longer allow negative concrete beliefs to spew irrational statements in an attempt to intellectualize or justify emotional reactions just because you think you *should* feel how you feel. Learn and apply the differences between criticism and analysis. There is so much of you left to discover and reveal.

Observe your thoughts, do not simply react to them,
and become the master of the silver lining.

RSA APPLICATION REVELATION

1) Pause. Ask yourself "What do I believe ?" (Components to Change)
- Keep the *"Principles of Change"* in mind

2) Write down your answer(s) "I believe ..." (Components to Change)
- Eventually you will be able to apply **RSA** in mind

3) Begin RSA Q&A's
- Begin by asking " Why do I believe ..."
to your answers in step 2
- Write down your response
- Repeat until concrete belief is revealed

4) Reframe your Belief Sentence(s)
- Remove each determinant word, negative narrative and both positive and negative irrationalities
- Begin your "New Belief Sentence" with the word **Remember**
- Use no determinant words, negative tone or narrative and end your Belief Sentence to be optimistic in outlook, but rational

5) - Apply **RSA** to your reframed Belief Sentence before adding it to *"Your Life Philosophy"*

DETERMINANT WORDS

These determinant words (and phrases) areas follows:

always, never, should, would, could (n't), can't, everyone, must (musterbation), have to, had to, supposed to, all the time, everywhere, assume, and expected.

These are redflags that you may be thinking irrationally

CHAPTER 9

YOUR LIFE PHILOSOPHY (LP)

No man or woman steps into the same river twice. For it is
not the same river and we are not the same people.
—HERACLITUS

S o far, we have spent time convincing you that your first reaction is prob-ably not your best response (unless of course that lion really is chas-ing you). We have focused on how, in the moment between the thought and the feelings, grasp the thought and hold it, examine it for it's true source. The source is often a negative concrete belief. Using the Principles of Change and the RSA tool, you will work to excavate and discard this destructive source. But the space where that negative belief was will not remain empty. Instinctively, you will work to fill it. How will you know what should replace it? How will you know if the replacement belief is bet-ter, is more true for you? Your written Life Philosophy or LP will tell you.

Like our work in capturing and reframing negative thoughts, this will be a deliberative process. It is not an emotional one. Making emotional choices sets you up for guilt, regret and shame, all of which are heavy con-tributors to your relapse into the old—old thinking, old feelings and old behavior patterns. This trio also paralyzes growth. You may even do this to yourself with intent to create a quick exit back. Cultivating, growing and using a well-defined LP reduces the probability you will make poor emo-tional choices that are not aligned with your personal truth. You will be making many choices soon and you cannot have the old decision-making process infecting and weakening your new framework.

What if I could show you an easy way to know your right choice when life needs you to choose? Would you be interested? Of course you would. I also have three quick steps to getting rich! I kid. Maybe *easy* and *right* are not the best words. More correctly, it is a way to know which choice is consistent with your truth and, therefore, minimizes the potential for regret, guilt and shame. You will still have to choose. Using the LP method will reduce the emotional infection in your choices and dramatically reduce the onset of guilt, shame, and regret. But it also increases your responsibility for the choice in that the choice was made with the right intention and reasoned, rational thinking. It does not mean that the choice will *always* be the *right* one; but being right is overrated. From our limited perspective in the present, we cannot know our good luck and bad luck, our good decisions and our bad decisions, sometimes for many years. What we thought was a fabulous opportunity may cost us more than we ever knew and the worst time in our life may produce good things we never imagined. But using your LP, you can know if the choice was true for you because it was made with minimal emotion and aligned with your beliefs, regardless of the outcome.

Perhaps you have other tools that help reduce the emotional fog in your decision-making process. Maybe you consider the pros and cons, weighing the good and bad consequences of your options. Some of you have been taught to begin any choice by weighing the options. This method actually leaves you more vulnerable to making a human choice based on emotion because you now see all the shiny possibilities in every option. This approach may be helpful but it also requires you to predict the future, predict how each choice may or may not impact you, your finances, your career, your health, your family. In the absence of a special gift of prophecy, you are as likely to be wrong as right and you may still be greatly influenced by your emotions. Regardless of your approach, just the need to make a decision, make a choice creates anxiety and toil. Under duress of a self-created emotional choice, stress emerges. This also begins harmful affects to your physical body by raising your cortisol levels, blood pressure and more. This increases the emotional potency, now biologically clouding your objective to choose by your truth and not from your emotions. People can even become addicted to the toil and begin to self create it for various reasons. Self importance creation, the feeling of normalcy in an intensive state and many other negative and positive rewards.

I bet you give great advice. Of course you do. Have you ever wondered why? It is because you have less emotion involved in the issue at hand. Less cognitive bias and more experience and wisdom. Throughout my time studying under him, Leo, often quoted his father. One of his father's truism that I repeat weekly to myself is *With all things cool, calm and benign, I'll solve anyone's problem unless it's mine.* Leo's would tell me I give great advice because when you are helping someone else, generally, you are about 30% emotionally involved in the choice. These numbers are not scientific. This varies given the *what* and *for whom* you are trying to help. This means you are using roughly 70% wisdom (your truth) when giving your advice to others. That is why you give great advice. Amazing how we can be so helpful to others so easily. The problem is when it is your personal choice. The percentages tend to reverse. The emotional involvement can become overwhelming. Try as you might to isolate the emotions from the decision at hand, it is difficult to really know how successful you have been. This is to remind you of the emotional investment you create in your own choices, and even why you might feel your choices are more complicated than anyone else's. Why you feel no one can understand except you. I mean, if you can solve *everyone* else's problems but yours, then they *must* be tougher, right? (sarcasm). It is this way because you can't choose wisely with so much emotion involved. How do then you reduce the emotion in your choices and decide from your personal truth? How do you set aside social constructs and environmental influence? Good friends and great mentors can be of tremendous help but their opinions reflect their own biases, their own life philosophies. You need an emotional filter that is your own. This is your LP. You are now in mentorship of yourself. Building your LP Foundation is your first assignment.

Taking the time to write your LP, especially when you are not facing an important decision, will reduce the emotional influences, pulling directly from the roots of your personal truths. This wisdom will now become readily accessible as you begin to refine your LP and use it to guide your decision-making.

What is your Life's Philosophy? You are living it but it may not make much sense. You are choosing, judging and labeling with it. It is revealed through your daily choices, internal and external dialogue, and in behavior patterns. Is that not scary to think about? You could be living by some secret philosophy on some conscious or subconscious level and you don't even know what it is? If you tell me you do not have a Life Philosophy, you could be living the *Fuck-It Philosophy*. What are the last two words you say to yourself just before that second you choose against your personal truth or better judgment and make an emotional choice? *Screw it* or *Forget it* if you happen to perceive cursing as offensive. You take the path of least resistance, away from anxiety, away from ownership, toward what is comfortable or even exciting. Two words allow you to make a purposeful, quick exit—all while somehow managing to internally shape the fall as having nothing to do with your choices. As if this approves stagnation or retreat. Finding or proving fault is a waste of energy. Oh yes, you are the captain of your ship, but it has no rudder, a ship left to the winds of chance and the currents of emotion.

Perhaps you do have a personal Life Philosophy. Is it directly useful in all life situations? Have you written it down and humbly and honestly examined it? Is it positive, rational and constructive or is it based in negative beliefs and painful experiences? Does it take into account others? Is it authentically yours or is it one you inherited from your parents or a memorized quote? My point, even if you have a LP, it is important to write it, to question it, to examine it, not once but often, grow it throughout your life. You are not the same person you were ten years or ten minutes ago. The Principles of Change remind us of the importance of humble self-analysis. What could we find that represents you more than your LP? If you use a well-thought-out rational LP, you can weigh your choices in life against it, not the outcomes of each choice. If it is a situational choice, then your LP will ensure your character, your truth remains intact. If your choice depends on the moment, then like many humans, you are weighing your options, waiting for the path of least resistance, and/or the most immediate reward. The fastest way to the perceived biggest piece of cheese. More than likely, you are not making the choice with genuine humility or from your place of truth. You will be less self-destructive if you choose based on your LP, even if the outcome is not the most rewarding or satisfying in the moment. Your truths become more easily accessible when you have your LP well defined. Imagine you begin to use your greatest strengths, you: your experiences, earned wisdom and rational thinking and perception control to conquer your greatest weaknesses, you.

If you choose based on the emotion of the moment or based on the potential outcome and not from your personal truth, most likely you will find yourself regretful or upset in the near future. At one time or another you made a choice and later said to yourself, *I knew it! Why didn't I listen to myself?* You chose against your truth and based your choice on the potential or even immediate reward or outcome of emotion. It may have possibly been the path of least resistance as well. Building your personalized LP and using it to make choices will dramatically reduce toil, stress, guilt, regret and shame. Using a personalized LP to make choices means no more long nights of toiling and wondering. No more lists! You just choose. When you can build your LP void of most irrationalities and fill it with your rational beliefs and optimistic personal truths, then you need only consult your LP for the personal truth choice to be revealed—no magic, no toil, no tricks. Only you will continue to allow the internal emotional volley to proceed after that.

Before you begin to build your LP, you have to remember that it, like you, is a process. Each experience in life, each new piece of knowledge and understanding, each competence gained, will add to my life.

As you write your philosophy, remember that words matter. Notice your chosen dialogue. The tone of your self-talk is choreographed by the words you choose. This shapes your life's narrative. Where would you presently categorize your life's movie? Is it a drama, comedy, horror, adventure, tragedy or hero story? Your answer may point you toward one or some of your negative concrete beliefs about yourself. The point is, choose your words carefully. Do not be concrete and criticize. Again, do not toil with your responses during any application of RSA. Simply Q&A. Your initial responses will be based in emotion. These are the windows to the irrational thoughts that will guide you to your Core and Concrete Beliefs, both positive and negative. Keep in mind the Principles of Change throughout each step of building your LP. Be humble and analytical as you cultivate your beliefs and the rest of your LP Foundation.

Building Your Life Philosophy

Step One: Core Belief Cultivation

Remember, your Core Beliefs are the answers three questions: What do you believe about the world? What do you believe about others? What do you believe about self? Applying RSA to each response will reveal and help you reframe three new powerful Belief Sentences, Belief Sentences because they will not just be positive wordplay. They will be powerful reframes written in the form of advice to yourself from yourself, advice pulled from your inner most truths. It's hard to deny your own advice, right? After you have applied RSA to these questions, three Belief Sentences will be revealed by you and become the first three sentences to your LP Foundation.

To more quickly assimilate the use of RSA, begin by writing all you think, state and respond with during its application to reveal your Core Beliefs. Write all your answers to these three questions as you apply the RSA Q&As. The first one and tenth one. Follow the RSA steps and write it down. Just ask yourself the question *What do I believe about the world?* Write your answers in one or two sentences only. Then ask why to that response. Do not toil here. You want your first emotional responses to be revealed. Over thinking here will cause a personal or social bias to slip in riding an emotion. You want to pull from your initial emotional reactions, your immediate thoughts, your most current beliefs, the ones that hit you first. Follow these. Do not toil.

Use RSA to meticulously analyze each of your answers quickly with more *why* questions. Do you see any determinant words, irrational phrases or negative dialogue such as *can't* or *try*? Do your *I believe* answers consist of rational dialogue construction and are they optimistic in tone? Cross out or strike through negative sentence structure, determinant words and what you believe to be irrational or pessimistic. Reframe your revealed concrete beliefs by beginning each of your new Belief Sentences with the word *remember*, as though you are leaving instructions for your future self. Shape your new Belief Sentence to be positive, optimistic but rational. Do not use any determinant words. Edit and build off your original written answer and all your following *why* responses. Q&A and reframe until revelation. Until your stated and written beliefs are optimistic and rational in thought construction. Don't focus on how they make you feel. Applying the RSA Tool to your three Core Beliefs (What do I believe about the world? About others? About self?) will reveal your first three Belief Sentences. The first three sentences to your Life Philosophy (LP).

You now have the beginning to your LP in three sentences, positive but rational advice from yourself you can call upon when life calls upon you to choose. Remember and use it when the world, others and self call any of these ideals into question. It even says *remember*. These are your thoughts, your beliefs, truths, wisdom and advice. How can you not listen to it? If you want to converse with someone to work through it, as I often do, be aware they will influence your choices whether they mean to or not, whether you know it or not. They can also help you if they know why and what you are trying to do. The number of sentences you can construct here is not limitless. Your three Core Belief revelations are to be kept to one or two sentences each. These are kept simple to reduce your human instinct to adapt and modify your own advice to certain situations. Less is more here. Simple is straight forward and reduces the *gray area* of the details. Remember to begin each new Belief Sentence just like this one, with the word *remember*. Apply RSA thoroughly to all of your reframes to ensure rational construction before adding any Belief Sentence to your LP. Even then, remember, your LP is a work in progress. You can change, revise and edit as you gain life experience and self-competence. Do not toil. Simply ask and respond. Write it down. Explore your thoughts like a humble mind traveler. You truly need to know what you believe about the world, others and self. Remember all your beliefs are built upon, and all of your thoughts are spawned from, your three Core Beliefs.

Step Two: Mentors' Wisdom

I will cover mentors more in-depth in Your I-to-E Inventory Chapter. For now, and to further build your LP Foundation, you will now choose and write down your go-to quote or quotes. In Step Two you can include your favorite philosophies from others'. Your mentors' words and advice will also be incorporated into your LP. These people are crucial because you have assimilated all or a portion of their perceptions and believe them to be useful. Pull from people you admire and respect. Write these quotes down under your three newly cultivated positive, but rational Core Belief Sentences. This is the second portion to your LP. There is no limit to the quotes you can add here. When you complete your selections, simply apply RSA to each quote that you have selected. Remember to use *why* questions when analyzing your selections. Remember, humility as you explore these quotes with the RSA Q&A's. Really question the rationality of your chosen quotes. Place no one person or quote on a pedestal. Reframe each quote by starting your customized version with the word *remember*. Use rational replacement dialogue if your analysis reveals it necessary. Remove what is proven to be irrational through RSA. Create a more optimistic tone in your reframed rewrites if necessary. Remember, even positive-sounding beliefs or sentence structure can be irrational.

For example, suppose you wrote *Remember to always tell the truth.* as a quote suppose that supports one of your three Core Beliefs. This sounds positive, but *always* is the red flag determinant word. It creates an irrational concrete absolute. A reframe example could be *Remember to be gentle with your honesty*. Be analytical and open up to the possibility that your *positive-sounding* quotes may be quite irrational. Analyze and explore because it can *always* sound good.

Your LP now includes advice from those you admire and respect, people who have positively affected your life and maybe even many others. This section will be cultivated further in this textual journey when you begin to build Your I-to-E Inventory. You now have a LP consisting of advice from yourself, your Core Beliefs reminding you what you truly believe about the world, others, and self and your mentors' advice, customized to align with your Core Beliefs.

Read your LP aloud from the top. The next sentence will be here when you're done. Does it sound like good advice? Of course it does! It is your advice! Feel free to remove or add new mentor quotes as your competence grows. Expand or revise your LP as life teaches you more about the world, others and yourself. Filter all new quotes, philosophies and beliefs with RSA before you add them to your LP.

Step Three: Complete Your LP Foundation

You will apply RSA to each of the remaining Components of Change, beginning in Chapter 10. Each time you apply RSA to a Component, a new rational and positive belief will be framed by you from your wisdom. Remember, the last step of RSA calls for you to add your newly reframed positive, but rational Belief Sentence to your LP. These Belief Sentences should align with your Core Beliefs. If they do not, keep applying RSA to the Belief Sentences or your Core Beliefs. Use RSA to be thorough not just before adding a belief to your LP, but especially before removing anything from your LP. This prevents you from revising your LP as a result of powerful or urgent emotions. Once you have worked each Component of Change with RSA, you will have completed the foundation to your LP. You will need your LP Foundation completed before you begin Your I-to-E Inventory in the last chapters.

Step Four: Test, Revise and Grow Your LP

Step Four is a reminder to use, test, work, grow and live your LP. Use your LP to make choices. Review the dilemma or choices at hand. Recite your LP and the right choice will be revealed. Consult your LP for all choices and especially before, during and after any pressing moment in life. This will come more quickly the more you use your LP to make life choices instead of human emotion or a list of pros and cons. Test your LP by using it to make choices big and small. If you refer to your LP and no direction is given for the choice or situation, this, too, is a positive. Perhaps no answer is your answer. Or continue to analyze the moment or component in question. Consult your mentors' advice. Seek experienced competence. Search for the competence. Many times, this will reveal potential new mentors or competence creators. Ask those you respect and love. Once you have gathered competence, apply RSA to the new competence variables and construct a new positive belief. Add it to your LP and test it. This is how you add and grow your LP. Next time, your LP will be armed with direct advice should this situation arise again in any fashion. This also helps you begin to see the *Obstacle Is the Way* to literally quote the book title from another Virtual Mentor of mine, Ryan Holiday.

You may reveal in time that advice you once gave yourself may not serve you as it once did. This happens because your life is changing. You change. Moments and choices bring other responsibilities and alter perceptions, needs, and desires. Do not feel hesitant to remove your advice from your LP, but only after you have applied RSA. This is not allowed to be done in order to fit perceived emotions in a given moment. Your LP is to be dissected and masterminded while not in the midst of an emotional fight. This is when you need to call upon your advice, not adapt it for your emotional needs. Stick to what is written when life hits. Revise your LP in a calm state only. Use your LP to stop the toil. It truly is the toil that destroys us. Remember, many times toil comes from us just not making a choice we know we need to make. Use the power of your own advice. Remember, your LP is not to be Play-Doh in the heat of the moment.

Become an active experimenter with our LP and remember: *test, test, test.* Test it by using it to make choices big and especially small. The small choices add up. This can be uncomfortable and difficult to do at first because your methods of decision making have been ingrained over your lifetime, concreted by your survival and life victories. You have been trained to simply feel and trust whatever arises from your emotions. At times, I still resort seemingly automatically to weighing my options by making mental and written lists. I consult a friend or mentor for an hour or so before I think of my LP. Side note on calling people for advice. You only call who you know will tell you what you already emotionally want to do. You are probably just using them for confirmation. Rather than first making a list or calling a friend or mentor, simply recite your options and do not include any pros or cons. Read your current LP aloud. If the right choice, the choice that matches your personal truth, does not become clearer after reading your LP a few times, remember, this, too, is a gift. You now know what competence to seek and what you need to add to your LP.

This is especially true after the outcome because you now have newly acquired life data. Add to your LP the new lessons life and the obstacles give you. Next time your LP will be better prepared for similar scenarios and you will not have to rely on memory or others. The experience will still have given you something. Experience and Competence. When life teaches you something through the problem opportunity route, as life does, add these lessons into your LP. Continue to grow your LP as you grow. Over time, this decision-making behavior begins to reinforce that experiencing difficult times is also an opportunity to grow, enhance, refine your LP and yourself. An optimistic attitude will begin to emerge because you know you will gain wisdom no matter the outcome. You know you grow wiser with uncomfortable experiences. You will begin to yearn to be constructively uncomfortable.

You cannot unlearn what you now know.
—Leo D'Anniballe

You may find yourself beginning at Step One more than a few times. Life-altering events and experiences tend to cause this more than our typical daily experiences, but never say *never*. This is not your stone tablet. Consider it written in pencil. If you can remain open to all perceptions and practice humility, you can learn to see problems, people and experiences as opportunities for you to be a student of life. Your experiences contain life nutrients of knowledge, but you must extract them.

You may find yourself in a place in time when a choice or behavior is immediate and you simply cannot apply RSA and your LP is not helping you. It is an overwhelming emotional rush in a moment. Perhaps the urgency has become too real, your emotions are overwhelming and you are trying to choose with thirty percent of your wisdom. When this happens to me, I reach for more of Leo's advice. First, pause and just be for a moment. Second, ask yourself if this is a top five in life? Meaning, if you had five days to live, would this be in the top five of your to-do or worry about list? If it is not, ask yourself why are you treating it as such? Understand, the lion you think wants to fight, is not real. If this situation is a *top-five* and you *must* deal with it now, take more of Leo's advice. *When in doubt, do what you would advise to the one you love most unconditionally.* This is great advice. Now I pass it on to you. Keep the person you love most unconditionally and would truly lay your life down for in mind. Simply do what you would advise to the one you love most unconditionally and immediately. Imagine that special someone is in front of you and tell them what to do. You will hear your wisdom right away. Listen to it. Do not toil with the emotion of it. Choose from your truth, not emotion.

> *When in doubt, do what you would advise.*
> —LEO D'ANNIBALLE

Your Life Philosophy will grow and change as you begin to change your perceptions by challenging your beliefs and responses. Continue to apply, analyze and revise your LP as life happens, as your self-competence grows and as people inspire you. Practice making even seemingly little choices with your LP like what to eat for lunch. If it doesn't answer it, revise and add to your LP. By the end of this book your Life Philosophy will have your truth and advice regarding the most important Components of your life including the little things as your life blossoms to its most authentic revelation. Your LP will filter your emotions, reduce guilt and shame, calm the mind, help you to take care of your body and help you make your next right choice in life. It can be passed down. Use your LP to stop toiling in the emotions and feelings you are creating. Reduce anxiety and begin to make choices from your truth, not emotion.

You will now begin to work the remaining Components of Change more individually, with less of my bias. You will apply RSA to each Component of Change to help you build your Life Philosophy Foundation. Again, you will need your LP Foundation and have a good handle on using RSA before you begin your I-to-E Inventory. This is the calm before the storm, the preparation to cultivate self-competence in order to grow authentic self-confidence. Remember, it is your negative concrete beliefs that you are hunting for. Passionately hunt for negative concrete beliefs. Once you are using and living your LP, applying RSA to control emotions and enthusiastically living your I-to-E Inventory, you may just be living your Cognitive Rampage. Until then, respect the process, but know that change can happen in a moment. The moment you change what you believe. Transitions are beautiful processes and will culminate in your Epic.

Life is a journey, not a destination.
—RALPH WALDO EMERSON

STEPS TO YOUR LIFE PHILOSOPHY

1) Apply RSA to your 3 Core Beliefs

Your LP Intro; After the Reframe

"Remember ..."

The World _____

Others _____

Self _____

2) Mentors Wisdoms

- Write down all your beloved, lived by, and passed down quotes, sayings, and phrases.
- Apply RSA to each, reframe them to be positive yet rational, and now personalized for stronger assimilation.

Your LP with steps 1 & 2 applied

"Remember ..." - **Reframed and rational sentences**

The World _____

Others _____

Self _____

Quote Reframes _____

(Use as many _____

quotes as _____

you want) _____

_____

_____

_____

3) Complete LP Foundation

- Apply RSA to all "Components to Change" to reveal and reframe your Belief Sentences
- The culmination of your Belief Sentences is your LP Foundation.

4) Use it ,Test it, Revise it, Grow it

Length is limitless and this is not your stone tablet.

PHASE IV: COMPONENTS OF CHANGE

YOUR NUTRITIONAL BELIEFS

You are what you eat, to a point.

French physician and now removed *Father of the Paleo* and low-carb diets Anthelme Brillat-Savarin wrote, *Dis-moi ce que tu manges, je te dirai ce que tu es: Tell me what you eat, and I will tell you what you are.* Early in this book, we talked about all the factors that come together to make us who we are. Biology cannot be ignored. Biology may be more so affected by the environments, but it is also funded by the nutrition it receives, to a point.

Biologically, your change starts with an assessment of your current health, frequented environments, and your nutrition. This is your biological front line, where your physical change begins. Most health insurance coverage includes a low cost or even required no co-pay annual physical. Sadly, it is almost the only opportunity for you to take advantage of preventive medicine. Ironically, many unwisely neglect this preventive opportunity. Remember that word, preventive; you will hear it from me often. Perhaps we ignore it because of fear; we know there is something wrong and we just don't want to deal with it right now. Perhaps it is because you are certain it is a waste of time and money; you know you are in good health. But this physical is a key reference point, a baseline from which you take charge of your own health. It may also represent your best chance to win the fight, if it turns out there is one approaching.

I prefer Functional Medicine Practitioners myself, but insurance companies typically do not. They can be difficult to find, and many times are expensive, but worth every penny in my opinion. Many physicians are held by many corporate and financials boundaries. Not to mention, when you (a physician) are a hammer, everything is a nail. Whichever type of provider you choose, always do your homework. Unfortunately, there is no federal registry of practitioners, so they can lose their license in one state and move to another. Most state information on practitioners is now available online; you can enter the name to find out if there have been any complaints, any disciplinary actions, any lawsuits. This check is only basic information and in no way is indicative how well-informed or talented your physician is. There are also many websites and apps where you can get information on your physician's education and training as well as patient ratings. Again, not indicative of talent and mastery. Bedside manner and how polite they are to you does not mean they are the best. Perhaps you need one that tells you like it is and is more concerned with getting you healthy rather than your feelings, their quotas and bottom-line. Finally, talk to people, especially those in the field. Nurses are often the best sources for recommending excellent doctors (and avoiding the bad ones).

Most practitioners will allow you to complete the required paperwork ahead of time at your leisure or electronically, saving you time at the office and ensuring the information you provide is accurate and complete. Go in prepared. Write down any questions you have ahead of time; questions about any symptoms, questions about medications, questions about their approach to health and the science behind their philosophy. I would urge you to go beyond even the thorough physical. Dr. Rhonda Patrick, again, is a good source to find out exactly which tests you will want to request that go further. Test more than once and have each test result peer reviewed, so to speak. Meaning get retested and review with other professionals from different fields of training. You will more than likely have to request the tests that go beyond the basics and testing typically suggested by professionals and that most insurance will cover. Some tests can even be done over the Internet. If you have insurance, more than likely your insurance will not cover any test if you do not have a supporting medical condition or symptoms. This is called reactionary medicine. The approach currently in place both medically and mentally in the United States. If your annual physical, or your body indicates any concerns, follow up! Follow the appointment with extensive research. Get other professional opinions, using a specialist if appropriate (and doing your homework on the specialist the same way you did it for your chosen practitioner). If it is safe for you, I recommend avoiding medications until all organic and holistic efforts have been competently exhausted for proper periods of time. The days of simply accepting the practitioner at their word and wisdom is over. You can believe that.

The downfall of our healthcare system is that it requires illness and diagnosis first; this is reactionary medicine at its finest. It reinforces the idea that we don't deal with our health until something is wrong. Thorough testing and regular physicals are the beginning of taking control of your health, the baseline that you need to know and monitor. But that's not the end of the story. That's just the beginning. You need to become preventive in your health, not reactionary. Nutrition is possibly the first catalyst for immediate change. You can begin your change with the food you choose to ingest. This affects your mood, mind and body. You will create a new belief foundation to nutrition shortly.

Nutrition at its most basic is about eating healthy food. You can fight early onset of many genetic predispositions with an individualized nutrition and (if needed) supplementation regime. There are multiple ways to begin the process of discovering what nutritional intake will best serve your biology. You can certainly test and retest nutrition on yourself. This is referred to as a form of *Bio-Hacking*. This is an emerging practice that many healthy and successful people insist on practicing. You can also start with a nutritionist or even an endocrinologist. There are holistic practitioners and other trained professionals as well. If you start with someone, start with a fully trained person or team who focuses on nutrition. Nutrition is an individualized practiced in my non-scientist opinion. This knowledge is worth every cent if you can afford it up front. Save for it if you cannot. Being able to adjust your body's intake to match more closely what it is your body is lacking, and even prefers, will reduce present suffering and prevent suffering later in life. The possibilities are evolutionary.

I am an enthusiastic supporter of eating organic if possible. If it comes out of a window, cooks in or comes out of a box or can, removes rust and would survive a nuclear attack, it is probably not good for you. If you have been eating poorly for any length of time, you may also be fighting biological and neurological addictions found in things like sugar, carbohydrates, and, I love this one, *other natural flavors.*

I will forgo the side-by-side comparison of costs-to-portion ratio to prove it is a myth that eating this way is too expensive. Consider the short-term and especially, the long-term health costs associated with over-the-counter treatments for symptoms and potential medical impacts of long-term consumption of poisons and *other natural flavors* found processed foods. Account for any and all prescription medication needed now or later in life. Add the damage they do over time to your body, increased medical visits and risk for early onset of diseases for which you may have predispositions. These costs are astronomical, financially, emotionally and physically, compared to eating as organic as possible. Eating healthy is not even close to the actual cost of not eating healthy overtime. Please understand that there are minimal requirements to legally use the word *organic* on a product. It can vary with certain products and certain states; for example, it may be legal to call a product organic when only 70% of its production actually is organic. The word *natural* means nothing. Do your homework.

Proper nutrition is preventive physical and mental health and can reduce or eliminate many symptoms and medical issues. It also saves money, pain and strife. You may notice many changes as you properly feed your body. Your mind will function faster with clearer thinking and an increased insight. Your energy begins to blossom. Your irritability will reduce as you are able to better manage your mood. Chronic pain will subside. You can expect to sleep better. Know your body's limits and requirements before diving into anything. The research is out there, good and bad. It is real food you are after, what your body was made to utilize, not this society of carnival food.

I will suggest a few basic ideas for those who may just be thinking about or starting to eat healthy and organic for the first time. I limit what

I advise because the idea is for you to cultivate your own interest(s) and to seek out what works best for you. These are basic. First, ignore the word *natural*. Again, this is a marketing trick to make you feel better. It has no legal meaning and, in fact, may be a sign they are lying to you. I take that personally, trying to trick me into feeding myself or my daughter poison!

Virtual Mentor Tim Ferriss, and author of *The 4-Hour Body*, gives a very easy-to-implement tip. Start by removing one processed food from your routine and replace it with one healthy food per week. Replace soda with cucumber-filled water. Remove fast food one week and replace it with a salad you made at home with local or home-grown vegetables. Change is a process revamped one choice and one behavior at a time. Respect the process of change in changing your nutrition. If you believe it to be difficult, it will be.

Many practitioners and professionals will tell you to let go of the three- meals-a-day routine and eat about every two to three hours to keep your energy balanced and your metabolism going. While others will tell you this almost guarantees obesity. Others will tell you to stick to *The Healthy Big-3* (three meals a day) and keep your snacking limited to none, and never after 9pm. Or is it 10pm? Wait it's 8pm or after 10 hours, right? See what I mean. There are also methods that propose the opposite of this idea, like intermittent and routine fasting. I intermittently fast and some days I eat every two to three hours or stick to the big three meals a day. I believe we are finally ceasing with the calories in calories out idea as the foundation. We now know it is not only about the number of calories necessarily. Potentially more importantly, it is about what kind of calories. In my opinion, choosing between 1,200 calories of bad food and 2,000 calories of a balanced and organic menu is no choice; the 2,000 balanced and organic calories win. Remember, food is fuel. That is my philosophy.

Fuel yourself with actual food. Remember before seeing a practitioner, build a list of questions to maximize your time. Do not just be fed information. Be prepared. While researching ahead of time, go where your interests take you. There are many aspects of nutrition, many ways to individualize your nutritional weapon. Be diligent in your test results. Review the results with your professional in-depth and ask direct questions about follow-through or eating adjustments. There is no magic pill! Yet. Ask what you can do and be a helpful part of the team. Do not robotically respond to their suggestions. Consume and engage your individualized nutrition regime through your internal beliefs and newly acquired biological competence, not your cravings. Food can be a harmful addiction as well.

You may go to your physical, take the tests, study nutrition, see a professional and choose the best nutrition path for you. You may understand and grasp the concept or importance of taking the best care of yourself when it comes to nutrition, but lack consistency or follow-through. This may be because you have this knowledge tied to a negative concrete belief that more than likely is being reinforced with your daily or cycling irrational dialogue, hence, your possible perpetual stagnation or history of inconsistency in this particular component of life. Action depends on your concrete beliefs, beliefs from which you carve your thoughts that create your feelings toward nutrition, resulting in your inaction, action or consistency. Change and individualized optimization in the nutritional component is what you are seeking. You will need to identify and challenge your current associated concrete beliefs beyond the initial emotional, intellectualizing and irrational dialogue. Stay humble. H=C Principle of Change.

I will borrow the cliché that eating healthy is a lifestyle choice. It is daily choices made from concrete beliefs you hold to be fact about food, you, your life, and the world. Your beliefs perpetuate your lifestyle and your present state is evidence of your beliefs, not others or your situation. What you believe about nutrition perpetuates your eating habits. If your eating habits are flawed, your concrete beliefs are flawed. Find that negative belief or perhaps that irrational belief. If you can't, you may simply lack the competence in your biology to be confident and enthusiastic that eating healthy will or won't make a difference. You may not believe it is as important as you know it to be. If you eat and live a healthy lifestyle, I would venture to say your beliefs about taking care of your body and health are rational, optimistic and ring of enthusiasm due to a level of competence. This competence reinforces positive concrete beliefs that continue to deliver rewarding life experiences. Even here, remember, it is about balance. If being healthy is not a part of your current lifestyle, I believe it is because you are creating negative dialogue to reinforce your irrational thinking based in negative concrete beliefs about food, nutrition and possibly self.

I will use my own life example to illustrate how I used RSA to cultivate a new belief regarding nutrition, more specifically eating organic. Trust me; I used to ridicule all the hype about organic food. My concrete beliefs were coming out in subjective statements I made about eating organic. I was stating my beliefs as though they were fact. I intellectualized and verbalized connections of this organic sales pitch to capitalism, advertising and marketing. This concrete belief kept me a denier, strongly rejecting the (rational) idea that eating naturally existing food was, in fact, better for you! Wtf right? This belief kept me eating poorly, despite all my *exercising*.

My best friend then, Danny, nicknamed me *Tubby*. For someone who thought he knew a lot about nutrition, my 240-pound thick, linebacker body sure didn't show it. I knew I was strong, I could trace my muscles, but was I healthy? I knew that subjective concrete statements declared as fact, the frequent use of determinant words, meant there was a potential for a lack of humility and a chance to learn something. At a minimum, I knew the statements I was making were not facts. This is where I began my questioning of my own beliefs about eating organic by applying RSA in a spirit of humility. I had no real basis for my beliefs and statements about the organic movement, no real experience eating this way. So why am I making such statements as fact? Performing RSA revealed I needed to seek competence in the matter of organic food and experience firsthand what I believed to be new marketing and just a fad.

The questioning of my beliefs with a humbled curiosity began to build an interest in this *trend*. I sought competence from research and those more educated on the topic. Seeking competence creates influential moments that can shatter concrete beliefs in less than a second after acquiring real competence through experience. After absorbing some tough facts, I reframed my original concrete belief to state *this organic movement may hold some benefits after all.* Even this slightly evolved belief allowed for growth. This mild interest grew into a confident belief because of the competence I sought and experience I gained. Small moments of experience fueled my desire for more competence. This eventually pushed me to act. I lost 60 pounds in three months with just my nutritional changes. No weight lifting or cardio. After I lost the weight I began with more of a biomechanical approach to training, centered around martial arts and the science based approach of *Functional Patterns* founded by my friend Naudi Aguilar. My daily body pains and aches from years of playing football and nearly twenties years of weightlifting began to disappear; even the lower back pain I feared required surgery subsided and is currently no more. More on this in the next chapter. My psoriasis all but vanished. My chronic IBS subsided within two to three weeks. Heartburn and Tums went in the first week and I could time my *healthy releases* almost to the hour. I slept better and longer than I ever have in my life. I felt amazing all day. My energy and focus seemed to double within a month. Changing my nutrition and severely limiting my intake of sugars, synthetics and genetically modified foods changed my daily life. I have not put back on one pound and it has been nearly three years. Not one previous symptom described above has returned. This three-month experience was started just by catching my determinant red-flag verbiage, suspending my concrete belief, applying RSA which generated a mild interest I choose to pursue. Passionate denial, evolved into a passionate dedication. I fed myself with daily competence and experiences that led me to be entirely enthusiastic. I even became certified in health nutrition. This experience reminded me I still knew nothing. Had I not been willing to question my initial concrete belief, think what my body, my life might be like today.

Trust me, the first two weeks were not comfortable. Cravings and addictions kept my mood irritable. My head thumped constantly for the first three days. All this reinforced how poisonous all I had been ingesting really was! Silver lining: after about two weeks, I felt as if I had coffee on an IV without the side effects. My energy was organically high! My body no longer held portions of my thoughts captive. I was freed from my body in a sense. A moment of exercised humility challenging a personal belief led me to seek genuine competence. This gave me experiences that changed my body and my mind forever.

Now it's your turn. Use RSA to reveal and reframe any and all negative concrete beliefs you may have about health and nutrition. Start by asking, what do you believe about nutrition? Write down your answer beginning with *I believe*. Now proceed to the RSA Q&As step. Continue until you reveal your negative concrete belief(s). Remember, the determinant words will give it away. Reframe the belief(s) by starting your new sentence with the word *remember*, just as you did for your three Core Beliefs, when you first began building your LP. Shape the narrative of this nutritional advice to match the essence of your Core Beliefs in your LP. Complete your reframed Belief Sentence to be optimistic and leave out all determinant words. Once you trust that you have reframed your new belief(s) to these guidelines, add the newly framed positive belief(s) about nutrition to your LP. You have now started a personal LP about nutrition. Expand this portion of your LP if you see fit (excuse the pun). Add when and what to eat. Hell, apply RSA to your thoughts about cravings and then add something to your LP about cravings that hit you. You will now have a cognitive tool to help you battle cravings and avoid the toil and potential future self-shaming. I am finding it is better sometimes just to go all in on the food craving and saturate the desire rather than raise my cortisol levels trying to resist for long periods of time. Disclaimer: This is not professional advice, just something I've been bio-hacking personally after a conversation with Naudi Aguilar.

Stop toiling and leaving yourself vulnerable to the emotion of the moment. Recite your LP multiple times if necessary. Cultivate the competence, a new positive and rational belief from your truth. Allow this new belief to replace and replay until it becomes automatic in your thoughts. Automatic thoughts have a negative connotation. But if the thought cycling is rational, positive and optimistic and is based in your positive Core Beliefs, why not allow it to run automatically? When these thoughts are replaying, what feelings are you now perpetuating? Exactly. That is the power of you. Optimize your Nutrition Component of Change by adding competence and daily experience. Build your new grocery list, form new habits and daily menus and transform your kitchen to quality over quantity. You will also see this will take up some of that lazy time. You will have to shop more than once a week to avoid spoil and waste. This will help you avoid one of reasons for relapse to the old: boredom. It will require you to skillfully shop and prepare your food again. This is constructive time replacement. Hell, replace your addiction to bad foods with healthy eating and movement. There's nothing wrong with that in my book.

Beware of online information presented as research or fact. Check the validity of the sources. It is murky water when determining fact or fiction, true science, peer reviewed or conjecture. Read the labels on the food you are eating and check the new ones you have chosen, too. They even will put phrases that read as healthy but have no impact in that particular food such as *Gluten Free* or even *Non-GMO*. They are looking to gain a customer. You are looking to gain competence and build your nutritional competence through experience. It may take a few weeks to find foods you can tolerate or enjoy. Let your taste buds, stomach bacteria and brain adjust accordingly. This is the adventure and learning process. Learn to enjoy it. Take it as them challenging you with a game of *Find The Poison*. Remember, whatever nutritional routine becomes your truth, be sure it is healthy. It is likely your body is not use to these new foods, new eating approach so don't be discouraged too soon. You can experience terrible physical and mental withdrawal symptoms the first few weeks. Let the body change. Let the mind soak up the nutrients. Eventually you will actually look at the old unhealthy food and your body will respond with a *Hell, no*! Your body talks to you if you just listen. Eventually it will crave what you have now trained it to crave; water, minerals, greens, real glucose from fruits, and not chemicals made in labs. Feed your body right so your mind can run right. It is where you biologically and behaviorally start. Your body is the most amazing instrument you will ever own.

CHAPTER 11

YOUR MOVEMENT

The body can reflect how you are treating your mind
and how your mind is treating your body.

I generally do not like to make such a staunch distinction between the mind and body as they are one. But I believe the mind cannot operate to its full potential if the body is not as healthy as biomechanically or biologically possible. If your body is polluted, stagnant or simply not properly maintained, then your mind will function accordingly. Your spirit and emotions are left to bear the burden of a malnourished body and an impaired mind. You are unbalanced. If you are constantly worried or unsure about your health or medical issues, your mind cannot work beyond the present state; your body is holding it captive. The body can reflect how you are treating your mind and how your mind is treating your body. Take control of your mind by beginning to treat your body better and vice versa. Your nutritional beliefs, the regime you construct are key factors to your success. But moving your body functionally and properly is another key factor. Yes, that age-old talent we evolved to do so wonderfully, forgotten or neglected by many, is an essential part of our humanness. You have to move with effort and purpose daily.

Many times, both nutrition and movement fall by the wayside. Sometimes it just seems that life gets in the way. But you may also hold negative concrete beliefs about both, and believe other more important responsibilities call upon you.

Apply RSA to the Movement Component exactly as you did to the Nutritional Component of Change. What do you believe about movement, or the term you've notice I do not use, *exercise*. Write this belief down. *I believe...* Self-analyze. Do not self-criticize and intellectualize. Perhaps the negative concrete belief emerges, the belief that *I never have time to exercise* or *I've never been good at exercise* or *I tried to enjoy exercise*. These statements are partly why I do not use the term *exercise*. In my perception, it is associated with a chore, and who wants to do chores? Movement to me is a given. Of course I move, I am human. Remember, to move functionally for the length of my life. That is my philosophy.

Refer back to the negative concrete beliefs above that many hold regarding exercise; notice the punctuation in these concrete beliefs? These are statements of perceptions as though they are facts drenched in negativity and self deprecation. They are statements of feelings as though they are unchangeable. Remember determinate words like *never, always and try* are *red flags* that the thinking more than likely is irrational. These are obvious irrational and negative beliefs that limit your possibilities, keeping you paralyzed with irrational mental poison, intended to keep you still or performing injury causing movements. If you are keeping a humble attitude and the Principles of Change in mind, then you know that if you truly believe yourself not to have time, that will be so indefinitely. If you have a concrete belief that you *never enjoy exercise*, that *you've never been good at anything that requires physical movement* and that *you hate exercising*, then you will sabotage any efforts to change your routine. Are you awfulizing exercise? I know I did. That is why I changed my belief and perception. Hell, I changed the word itself!

Can you practice the humility to admit that you may just lack competence in health and proper movement? Remember, it is competence and the experience that leads to confidence and sustained enthusiasm. Remember, it is your own beliefs driving your thoughts that are holding you back.

Investigate your statements of subjective fact. Making irrational negative statements means you can continue to believe it is not your fault and you don't want to be wrong, do you? Busy is better, right? Remind yourself that your thoughts create your feelings, and feelings influence behavior. *I never have time to exercise* is a negative concrete belief that is reinforced because your chosen dialogue is meant to awfulize and substantiate your inaction. You believe yourself to be busy, so you are. Then you reinforce this belief with your chosen internal and external dialogue. You are creating emotions that confirm your negative belief about how much time you have and, perhaps more importantly, what the priorities are for your time.

The challenge to consider the time you have for learning and applying healthy Functional Patterns of movement is not intended to minimize the demands of a single mother or a caregiver of an elderly parent or disabled person. These are real and exhausting responsibilities, emotionally and physically. But these enormous responsibilities make taking care of you even more important. I am asking you to consider a new belief, even if it is only to do more research or more experimenting with exercise or movement of any kind. I am not asking you to change your belief from hating exercising or feeling guilty about exercise to loving it. Change the belief to something rational for you. If you have children, use the love you have for them to model a healthy lifestyle. If time with your children is another factor, find a way to move with them; take a regular walk together or physically play together. Children can be good extrinsic motivation; an exterior motivator for change, just the fuel you need to reframe your negative concrete belief about exercise. You need to frame a new positive belief and thinking process directly related to movement. Perhaps, *Remember, maintaining my body with proper movement is one of the biggest responsibilities as a parent to model and teach my children.* As a parent myself, I ask you, are there more important earthly responsibilities than your children's health? If your child is struggling with low energy or is overweight, being a positive, but active role model is invaluable. Not by telling, but by doing. Helping them understand their bodies, finding fun ways to move with purpose may inspire enthusiasm. Teach them, learn with them and be open to their suggestions. Work together. Living your negative beliefs or nagging, judging and demeaning your children will only create new negative beliefs in them, not just about exercise and nutrition, but about you and themselves. I cannot overstate the important of changing your negative beliefs about movement and nutrition for your children, your family and especially yourself. Being healthy and active allows you (and your children) the ability to access all life has to offer and to enjoy it longer with reduced suffering. As with all change, it begins with what you believe.

Conclude the Movement Component of Change analysis using RSA. Reframe any negative concrete beliefs about exercise or proper movement. Find a way to structure your dialogue to tap into your rational and positive concrete beliefs. Revise, rewrite and reframe until you reach the requirements for addition to your LP. Your LP now contains your advice and philosophy about self, others and the world. It also includes your mentors' advice. Feel free to add any healthy lifestyle quotes or mentorship advice here as well, but only after you have applied RSA to them. You can now consult your own advice to remind you of your personal truths about nutrition and movement. Your advice to self. Rational and authentic beliefs for real and lasting change. You will no longer be a product of your environment. Your environment will be a product of you. Your LP and RSA will not let you hide behind irrational and negative justifications. Dig in and root out your negative concrete beliefs about movement. Learn and practice functional and healthy movement. Reshape your fight song and go to war for your health, for your kids, for your happiness and for your change.

Warning: An extrinsic motivation will bring you to the water, but only an intrinsic motivation will keep you drinking the water. There are millions dead along the water's edge. Your children may motivate you initially but my hope for you is to find an internal drive that does not rely on others. Your children will grow up, hopefully with positive concrete beliefs about movement and nutrition. Find what will keep you moving and enthusiastic in the long run.

CHAPTER 12

YOUR SLEEP BELIEFS

Do not be willing to lose sleep to better your life.

Sleep sustains your life. Losing sleep diminishes your life. Every aspect of your life. The most important part of your daily routine is sleep; it is not success, not accomplishing daily goals. Good nutrition and functional movement cannot compensate for lack of sleep; there is no substitute for a consistent and maintained sleep routine. There, that covers it; end of discussion, no debate or salesmanship here. Done. I could rattle off stunning facts and research about sleep, but instead I will try to simply construct one straightforward paragraph in the hope that it smacks you in the head hard enough—and well, maybe a little salesmanship.

Lack of proper sleep can cause psychosis, delusional thinking, impaired perception, emotional instability. It retards cognitive functioning and your thinking is not to be trusted. Your memory becomes vague and your mood can become hostile and/or withdrawn. You may even feel symptoms of paranoia. Poor sleep increases the severity of most, if not all, medical and mental health diagnoses such as chronic pain, depression and anxiety disorders. You will cycle faster if you suffer from bipolar. Severe depressive symptoms arise from poor sleep and begin to sprout thoughts you may have never even joked about. Your body can begin to display the damage from lack of sleep in a paralyzed metabolism, wild and random cravings; periods of not eating and overeating will occur more often. If you have a predisposition to a disease or condition, lack of sleep can cause it to appear sooner than typically expected.

Simply put, continuous periods without good sleep kills you. There is a reason that sleep deprivation is an especially sinister form of torture; sleep is a biological requirement for all human beings. Synthetic sleep medications, whether over-the-counter or prescription, are not intended to be taken for life. They have been linked to increased risk of dementia. Holistic methods such as herbal teas and melatonin are much healthy substitutes. There are also many organic sleep aids, breathing and meditation methods for sleep assistance.

The power of you is the best medicine. In fact, the National Sleep Foundation and the Mayo Clinic are now recommending cognitive behavioral therapy, without medication, as an approach to lack of sleep. RSA, your LP, proper nutrition and movement will help correct many organic reasons for your sleep problems. Maintaining a consistent and healthy Sleep Routine can begin right now. If you have no trouble falling and staying asleep, identify your healthy pattern. Some research does indicate the number of hours of sleep can be different for everyone and changes for each person as they age, health conditions and level of daily activity. But if, like millions of Americans, you have trouble with good sleep, try this simple *Sleep Setting Formula* as a basic place to start. Look at your week and determine the earliest time you have to be awake and write it down. Find the day of the week you must remain awake the latest and write it down. If roughly seven to ten hours exist between these times, this is your new sleep schedule for the week. If not, you need to make adjustments or possibly work in a regular napping schedule. Track your sleep patterns for at least two weeks, along with what you were doing and what you have ingested two to three hours before you go to bed. Prepare, train or retrain your body. To the greatest extent possible, establish regular times for going to bed and for getting up into your routine. I would suggest eliminating blue light all together (courtesy of Dr. Jack Kruse), no screens prior to bed or while in bed and I would not suggest reading anything that stimulates your cerebral. Reading fiction before bed knocks me out like Mike Tyson in the 90s. Find a way to make your room dark; it is a natural biological trigger for sleep. Try not to work or study in the bedroom; make it your place for sleep and *other movements*. And if you don't fall asleep within 15-30 minutes of going to bed, get up. Don't stay in bed, staring at the ceiling, tossing and turning. When you get up, don't eat anything heavy, don't watch an action movie or read that self-help book. Do something that is calming, even boring. Then, when you feel ready, try going to bed again. Your life does depend on it.

Apply RSA in its entirety to reveal your concrete beliefs about sleep. Perhaps sleep was associated with laziness; perhaps sleep is associated with fears, nightmares (real or imagined). Use RSA and then do not forget to add your new belief regarding sleep to your LP. It is hard to fight your own advice when you can't manipulate it, when it is written down right in front of you.

Do not think you can make up sleep on the off days due to overworked days. You cannot make up for lost sleep. We are resilient human beings and our bodies can tolerate occasional or brief interruptions. But if sleeplessness is the state of your life, perform more research then a few taps or clicks to gain competence. Do not listen to the advice *You have to be willing to lose sleep to be successful.* Feeding your body with the right rest allows it to work for you, not against you. Sleep heals the mind, giving it time to process events in life and your past. Sleep is also believed to work out deep subconscious conflicts. Give it a chance to do so. Resting the body allows nature to work for you, not against you. In about two or three weeks of eating healthy, regularly performing Functional Patterns of movement and keeping a routine of healthy sleep, you will feel the difference. You can't argue the opposite until you've tried it.

Nutrition, movement and sleep are the triumvirate of health for your body. Warning: It can get worse before it gets better within those weeks. Short-term pain versus long-term pain. As you begin to move, you may experience aches and pains. Double and triple check the movements you are choosing are functional and healthy. Sleep may be difficult as your body sheds the toxins and your energy level begins to rise. Good sleep is very important during a transition and is as important as movement and nutrition. Your body is the most amazing instrument you will ever own. It is the most crucial do-it-yourself project that you will ever be assigned. It is the front line of your change, the first to tell you something is wrong, a very loyal weapon in your fight for change, once you can trust it. Find and protect your Nutrition, Movement and Sleep Components of Change as though your life depends on it. It does. This is more important than your bank account, the car you drive, your 401(k) and the school your children attend. What good is an absentee or dead parent? What good is a retirement if you are not here to enjoy it? What good is life insurance if your family has to use it to pay the medical bills you racked up before you dropped dead? If you are a parent, in my opinion, these three lessons, nutrition, movement and sleep, are the most important earthly functions of life. We teach and model them to prevent their suffering. Not career, education, money, status, performance, acquisition or accomplishment. But that is just my perception.

Your nutrition, movement, and sleep routines will help you fight most diagnoses, both mental and medical. It will also enhance the effectiveness of many mental and medical treatments. I believe proper and sustained nutrition, movement and sleep are not just parts of a healthy lifestyle, but are preventive healthcare treatments. These treatments are accessible for most people, bring minimal risk with the potential for great reward. They are treatments, tools and now a part of your LP and soon your Authentic Routine.

Health is wealth. When life happens—a job is over, a life partner moves on or the dice rolls snake eyes—no matter what, you have your health. This keeps you in the game, prepared to take on anything life has to offer you, prepared for any mental or physical opponent.

CHAPTER 13

YOUR DIAGNOSIS AND TREATMENT BELIEFS

I will solely concentrate on mental health diagnoses and treatments because this is my level of training and experience. Medical diagnoses are far out of my scope of practice. A World Health Organization report titled *Investing in Mental Health* found that around 20% of adults are affected by some form of mental disorder every year. About 3% of adults experience psychosocial disability caused by mental illness each year. That means that more than 74,000,000 people annually are impacted by mental illness and this is just what is reported. Due to the stigma of mental health diagnoses, many people do not seek help. Up to 15% of people seriously affected by mental illness die by suicide compared to approximately 1% of the general population. Mental illness is real. Mental health diagnoses are a different matter.

If you currently have not received a mental health diagnosis from a licensed professional, you will NOT be applying RSA in any fashion to this Component of Change. I do not want you exploring the possibilities of a mental diagnoses without cause. You will not use these components later in your I-to-E Inventory. However, I suggest you read on for a few basic reasons. Should the day arrive that you or someone you love are concerned about mental health implications or receive a mental health diagnosis, you will be able to do your part in the fight. If it is someone you care about, you may be able to assist a friend or loved one in finding the right path.

If you currently are being affected by a mental or medical health diagnosis, I want to begin with an important change in your dialogue before you apply RSA. Please stop speaking of yourself as though you are a diagnosis.

Rather, speak of yourself as being affected by a diagnosis; not that you are that diagnosis. You are not depressed. You are not an addict. You are being affected by depression. You are being affected by addiction. You don't say, *I am headache*, do you? You don't say, *I am cancer*. These are conditions that affect you. They are not you. When you use dialogue to label yourself as a diagnosis, this influences your feelings and behavior. This type of labeling and self-talk can create self-fulfilling prophecies and dramatic behavior changes over time. You may begin to act as you believe you should, simply based on your diagnosis. Just by saying certain words, remember, pictures appear in your mind. If you see yourself as a negatively created perception, then this is truly what you believe yourself to be as a person.

Try saying, *Hello, my name is Sam, and I am being affected by addiction.* This removes the personal definition and identification. *Hello, my name is Sam, and I am an addict* is a passive acceptance to being powerless in your own life and choices. I will use a Leo example to hopefully convince you to stop labeling and defining yourself to be a diagnosis, *to help you separate situation from self*, as he would say. If you were witness to a bully beating up a much smaller child would you be angry at the smaller child? I hope not. Your focus of disgust would be at the bully, not the child. Depression and alcoholism are just some of the bullies you may face in life. You are the one being bullied in this scenario. You are not the bully. Addiction is what is affecting you. It is not who you are. It is a bully. You would stand up to a bully, wouldn't you? As you now know, dialogue is crucial in the mental game of life. Do not continue to convince yourself that you are your diagnosis. Change your dialogue to separate situation from self.

After you have separated yourself from your diagnosis, you will be able to much more objectively question your diagnosis. Do not just accept it. Please understand that I am not-telling you that your diagnosis (or the need for one) is not real or accurate. I am not telling you to stop a prescribed regime that is working well for you. But if that is not the case, there are other options to consider. Bear in mind that diagnosing mental health is not an exact science, and is theory. It is more of an educated game of observation and comparison to subjective notions of normal or accepted behavior references. There is no scientific method of testing for depression or bipolar disorder, yet. Much of mental health diagnosing is based on self-report and observation by a trained professional. Both perspectives bask in the light of biases. There is also no clear-cut scientific method to test and prove addiction is present. This, too, is based on patient self-report and biopsychosocial assessments, compared still to a subjective normal. It is not like testing for the presence of cancer or diabetes. Even these medical diagnoses can be the result of false positives or human error. Think how much more vulnerable mental health diagnoses are to human error.

There have been many edits, removals and changes to volumes of the *Diagnostic and Statistical Manual of Mental Disorders (DSM)*, considered by most practitioners the standard of criteria for diagnosing mental disorders. Others criticize the DSM for trying to establish objective standards for problems that are tremendously subjective. The emphasis on specific criteria to define normal and abnormal feelings and behaviors, and the emphasis on a disease model that is cured through prescriptions have been the subject of much debate and controversy since its conception, and undergoing multiple foundational changes. A small group of trained professionals revise, add and remove as they see fit, based on peer-reviewed research and data. But the degree to which the data and the information provided is objective and scientifically supported can and should be questioned. I am sure this research is not skewed at all by financial influence or researcher bias. That is sarcasm. Corruption knows no bounds. In 2013, there was a major overhaul and complete restructuring of the *DSM*, to create the now fifth edition. Spectrums have been widened on nearly every diagnosis. The Axis system that was used for nearly a decade has been removed and replaced with severity levels and traits creating more room for subjectivity, in an attempt to bring together common criteria for accurate diagnosing. This also increased the number of individuals that now qualify for pharmacological interventions. These wide-ranging spectrums are used to fit a person into the closest possible category of possible diagnosis. Just now with severity spectrums. They try to combine these subjective notions with personal and family history, all as reported by the patient, to develop a mental health diagnosis. With wider spectrums, more people *qualify* for a diagnosis, for treatment, prescription interventions and while also now becoming subject to this advice for treatment more frequently. I wonder how that happened? Insurance companies require a diagnosis be administered for admission into any inpatient level of care, and for payment to be issued to the facility. You could potentially classify somewhere on the mental health diagnosis spectrum with the DMS-V-TR right now or at some point in your life. Be wary these days of any quickly administered mental health diagnosis. I am not saying bipolar, post-traumatic stress disorder, attention deficit hyperactivity disorder and other serious mental health diagnoses do not exist. I am simply saying there is currently not an exact scientific method to mental health diagnosing that is not affected by practitioner or patient bias.

In addition, much of the research on pharmacological interventions is funded by pharmaceutical companies who inform the doctors that are backed by special interest groups. Be wary of practitioners who immediately begin treatment with recommendations of pharmacological intervention, especially concerning your children. If a physician prescribes painkillers, anti-depressants, and other dangerous and life altering medications, like Adderall, after asking you a few questions and/or after filling out a questionnaire, get another opinion. You and/or your child may also be asked to fill out a basic assessment. A few minutes with a practitioner are not sufficient for any major mental health diagnosis of any kind to be rendered, especially bipolar, schizophrenia, schizoid-affective, major depressive disorder and attention deficit (hyperactivity) disorder (ADD or ADHD). These are the leading, popular diagnoses of our time. Many practitioners toss around and label people without proper assessment, observation, and a thorough history check. Remember, it is important a person be at their biological baseline before these diagnoses are considered. Meaning that overuse of drugs or medical issues have been eliminated, proper nutrition, movement and rest have been confirmed for a well-observed period of time and no overuse of drugs is presently occurring. By no means are you personally or parentally responsible or qualified for rendering or removing any diagnosis concerning yourself or your child in any sense. Even if you are trained, you hold a bias that distorts your assertion. But you know yourself and your child better than any practitioner, and while this knowledge may bias you, it may also inform you. You are responsible for double and triple checking all diagnoses and treatment recommendations with other qualified practitioners before accepting any of them to be accurate, the most beneficial and the lowest risk. Pharmacological interventions are risky, especially for children. Done properly they can also be life-enhancing or life saving.

Because you can frame behavior and give it a label does not mean it is necessarily abnormal or is an actual diagnosis needing intervention. If someone says you are crazy, ask them, *As opposed to what?* Technically, the maladaptive thoughts, feelings and behaviors must disrupt and negatively affect your bio-psycho-social functioning to classify an existence of a mental disorder; your biological, cognitive functioning and social relationships are negatively affected over a given time period. Again, *negative* can be subjective and is open to cultural and generational bias. Importantly, mental disorders cannot be issued or determined with the presence of synthetic influence to the person being evaluated. But this happens every day.

Unfortunately, we don't have a mental healthcare system; we have a mental disorder system. Your insurance company won't cover you getting help unless there is a mental health diagnosis. One example is Adjustment Disorder, meaning, in simplistic terms, that you are going through some shit. Perhaps this is just life and you messing with you. Even so, this is a mental health diagnosis and can qualify for a pharmacological intervention.

Most current mental health interventions are only as good as the belief the client has in its potential to be effective. Without a positive belief, most help just becomes noise and failed attempts. The prognosis of many medical and mental health interventions is affected by patients' attitudes and beliefs. If you believe something will work, it can help tremendously, sometimes regardless of whether it has been proven scientifically to be effective or not. The placebo effect can be highly effective, too.

Your beliefs regarding your current professional mental health diagnosis or *googled* self-diagnosis play a key role in your progress, in your growth. At one end of the spectrum, your beliefs can impact the truth of the diagnosis or the severity of the diagnosis. But these beliefs can also impact your chosen path of treatment. Explore the emerging new research and treatments concerning any diagnosis currently affecting you. More than likely, you will discover new holistic treatments, nutritional weapons, movement defenses, cognitive efforts and behavioral interventions that are revealing amazing results and even cures, some fact and some fiction. But they exist.

Pursue competence in your diagnosis and chosen treatment regime. Question and analyze all personal concrete and associated beliefs regarding your current diagnosis and treatment protocols. More than likely, there are environmental, behavioral, nutritional, and mental changes you can begin to work on before or while receiving medication. At some point, you may end up eliminating the use of most or even all current synthetic prescriptions and medications. Please do not simply cease taking your current medication(s). This can have very harmful effects. You still need to consult your current practitioner concerning any possible medical or mental health diagnosing or misdiagnosing and the implications of discontinuing any medications as well as implementing any nutritional and movement changes, and alternative treatments. Ask about *titrating*, or gradually reducing or replacing medications with more holistic approaches. Ask which medications are meant for your entire life, which are for maintenance or to address temporary issues and which are purely optional. Put your work in and do not become entirely dependent on a synthetic support if possible. Be wary of chemical incarceration, that is becoming addicted to the process of treatment with pharmaceuticals without exploring the potential for an alternate healthy life. If you believe yourself to need something, then it will remain so; explore and consider an alternative.

Again, if you currently do not have a mental health diagnosis of any kind or pending, then do not perform RSA on these components and do not utilize these components in your I-to-E Inventory. I do not recommend you begin to analyze yourself for possible mental or medical diagnosis. Avoid this behavior. Do not create what is not there. If you currently are diagnosed or are being affected by a mental health diagnosis, proceed with applying RSA as you did previously to nutrition, movement and sleep. Begin by asking what you believe about your current mental health diagnosis and treatments. Proceed through the application of RSA. Seek competence in your diagnosis and available treatments. Be careful how you search for competence in diagnosis and treatments. Searching to prove you have something is different than searching to prove you do not. For example, if you are thinking about buying a Corvette, suddenly you may begin to think you are seeing more Corvettes. There has not been a sudden influx of Corvettes in your town. You are just looking for them. Beware the source of your competence as well. Go deeper and prove you do not have whatever it is a friend, commercial, or practitioner has told you that you are possibly experiencing. Do not try to prove you have anything. That is the practitioner's role.

I am stressing the importance of diligent competence when considering mental health diagnoses, medications, treatments and advice due to the lifelong implications that misdiagnosis and mis-treatments could have on your life. It is rare a psychiatrist or physician spends more than five minutes with you these days. They are being pressured to hit patient quotas and are also trapped in the corrupt mental and medical healthcare system. They do not bear all the blame. Unfortunately, the day of taking your doctor at face value is over. Many face career, revenue and legislative influence to perform by certain protocols, pedal specific medications and treatments. Beware. Find one that will listen to you, not talk down to you, and is conservative in diagnosing. I urge you to seek a practitioner who does not reach for the prescription pad first thing. What's most important is that you are well-informed and know what to expect of a competent practitioner. Good luck. Do not quit looking for the right help. They do exist.

By no means am I suggesting you can competently believe or necessarily in every case eat or exercise away or even prevent serious mental and medical health diagnoses such as schizophrenia and cancer. I am saying there are most certainly no harmful side effects. I am saying that you need to be more vigilant in your own mental and physical health, more than your doctor, more than your family, and more than you have in your past. You need to be on the team while questioning everything. If you have tried every holistic route and have resulted to prescription interventions, then you need to track and work this intervention style properly, meaning combined with holistic and psychological therapies and when your doctor asks you *how the new medication is working?* They need more than an *It's OK.* Keep a detailed journal and use a one-to-ten rating scale:

> I woke up at 8:00 a.m. and felt great—nine. I took my supplement or medication as directed and an hour later I was half-asleep with a serious headache and belly pains—three. It's now three hours after taking the new supplement or medication and I feel like a seven.

Put in the work. Do not be a pawn in your health. Do not continue to be the hamster in the wheel. Fully participate in your diagnosing process and treatments by asking questions. See counteracting practitioners. See a holistic practitioner and a medical model practitioner. Learn both or all the arguments and research yourself. Simply being told you have a mental disorder does not make it so. If you do, you will need to be competent and confident in treating it. You play the most important role in overcoming it. Not the practitioner and more than likely not the pill.

If you become competent in your diagnosis and treatment, you can be more confident it is accurate and more enthusiastic in treating it. You will have a better attitude and be a stronger addition to *Team Heal Your Ass.* No more fighting about whether to take medication or not, the on-again/ off-again process. Gaining competence requires more than simply two or three opinions of smart friends and a few *googled* articles. Pursue research from qualified sources. Read books on the topic, not just brief social media posts and taking your parents' or neighbors' experience as the only way. Remain humble and open in your research. Set out to prove you don't have whatever they or your past has told you is affecting you. Warning: Denial can be a strong adversary, as well. Beware of self-denial. Denial of a mental disorder can be just as deadly. This will come, too, in irrational statements as you seek competence. Observation and self-awareness fights denial. Humility shatters cognitive dissonances.

The goal is to become competent in your possible diagnosis or misdiagnosis so you can be confident when applying chosen treatments or ending others. You need treatments you can be enthusiastic about working and applying, treatments found in your competence search that build a confidence in you that the selected treatments match your given diagnosis and beliefs, if there truly is one. Again, be careful with labels. Thinking patterns and behaviors attached to given labels can begin to take on self-fulfilling prophecies.

You will discover movements and foods that can assist you in your fight with certain diagnoses, enhance treatments and improve prognoses. The possibilities are endless in what you can discover and implement in your life holistically and scientifically. Exercise the principles and apply the Tools of Change. Apply RSA now to your current diagnosis and current treatments. With this advice added to your LP, you can better keep yourself on your road to recovered, healthy, and happy.

If you are not willing to talk about the impossible,
then you are planning for the inevitable.

CHAPTER 14

LIFESTYLE AND YOUR PEOPLE, PLACES AND THINGS

Be aware in your environments, because they do give back (influence)

Your external and internal environments have the most influence on your development. Fortunately, they may also be the factors over which you have the most control as an adult. Your internal environment is what you believe and how you think, what you believe to be true about the world, others and self and how you process information. Your internal environment is what you think and feel. External environments surround your daily life and have influenced your development even before birth. Your mother's environments and experiences while you were in the oven baking influenced your development, the culture and home you were raised in, the environments you experienced, frequently and even just once. Your external environments are what you have experienced in your life with various people, places and things. The epigenetic influence.

The concept of your internal and external environments is pretty straightforward. However, the interaction between them is anything but straightforward. It is how your internal and external environments interact and duel that will be the focus here. Just as your internal environment shapes and influences your external environments, your external environments have and continue to shape your internal environment. Your external environments help form your concrete beliefs; we know how important these beliefs are to your thoughts, feelings, choices and behaviors. For purposes of this discussion and your LP, I will use the term lifestyle; for purposes of the I-to-E Inventory, we will focus on the people, places and things in your current routine. Your LP needs to have beliefs about your lifestyle. You shape your lifestyle based on perceived needs. These perceived needs arose from many sources but are based in your internal beliefs. Even basic interests can become wants that can begin to evolve into perceived needs. You believe you need a lifestyle (external environment). This perceived need begins pouring and reinforcing your concrete beliefs, creating the internal environment necessary to live, reflect, and/or obtain the desired— no, necessary—lifestyle. You seek the people, places and things that help you define the lifestyle you perceive you need. The external lifestyle thus becomes your internal way of thinking. You allowed the external environment to mold your internal environment. Thus, the feelings and beliefs toward any chosen lifestyle suggest it is who you are. When your internal and external environments are aligned, you should feel satisfied, content, right? We know it is not that simple. We know that sometimes the lifestyle we believed we wanted and needed does not deliver the expected internal belief. Is it the belief or the lifestyle that is wrong? The answer to that question is one only you can answer. I will provide some examples in which you may see yourself. Use the examples when you humbly apply RSA to this Component of Change.

Perhaps you are living a lifestyle from your past, one you even swore you would never live. But an honest and humble examination reveals you have re-created a lifestyle similar to the one you came from or have even been trying to forget. You have the starring role in a lifestyle, providing you an external environment you are used to, one that plays to your life's narrative, a place where you perceive yourself to function better. Remember, your current skills (and lack of them) work in this type of lifestyle. It is what you are comfortable with. Even if this lifestyle re-creation is a war zone, you may have simply normalized it. You may find yourself actually wanting it, eventually believing you need it because your coping skills work here. Your beliefs create the lifestyle and the lifestyle begins to define you as you see yourself. You continue to tailor your life's narrative to fit the chosen lifestyle. The lifestyle thus becomes who you are. It is who you believe yourself to be, possibly even what you think you deserve or all you believe yourself to be worth.

An extreme example of this happens to millions of people who have (rightly or wrongly) spent time in prison. A person adapts themselves for survival on the inside; they are hypervigilant and learn the skills necessary to survive in a constant state of fear, submission, anger or dominance. Years in this war zone result in this thinking and behavior becoming normalized. Life outside the razor wire doesn't necessarily require such a state, but the person had to adapt their mind-set or internal environment to their external environment in order to survive inside. Not being so could cost them their life. When released, usually without education or skills to earn a living and no time to transition their thinking and behavior, they are asked to return to a world where the person they have been for years to survive is not acceptable. Eventually, they may find help and make a transition but most often they find the ugly part of their community where this behavior, this thinking, this lifestyle is normal, even rewarded. Many simply re-create the prison lifestyle on the outside or return to prison, where they feel they work, where it is comfortable. Yes, I said *comfortable*. The same can be said for active military and veterans, abusive childhoods and relationships. They can all be war zones you (unknowingly) re-create because you think you deserve it, because it feels normal, because you seem to just work in this lifestyle. It is rewarding you. It is who you are, right?

I will use a more general example to try to bring to life the duel of the internal and external environmental. An elementary school boy has arrived for his first day at a new school. The youngster barely knows his address, let alone who he is as a person. Confidence tends to elude most at this age. He has only been told over and over who he is supposed to be. Regardless of his socioeconomic status, his intelligence, his looks or his personality, on a basic human level, the boy just wants to feel accepted.

It comes time for lunch and the boy knows he will soon have to choose his seat. His fear escalates when he first gets in line for lunch. While in line he is constantly scanning the lunchroom for a safe place, a table where he thinks he can sit and be accepted (or at least ignored). But it is much more to the boy at this point in childhood development. As the boy exits the line with his food, what is he looking for? Perhaps kids dressed like him? A smiling face or inviting body language? Suppose someone calls out to him to come sit with them? This immediately gives the boy a reward, possible safety and acceptance. He quickly walks toward the invitation to acceptance. He will immediately begin to observe what his new environment looks like before his first step toward the call. With a few glances, he will decide whether this is friendly territory or perhaps a joke, a trap.

The potential consequences of his acceptance of that simple invitation are impossible to calculate. If the outcome of the invitation is positive, the clothes he is wearing that day may even become his favorite outfit or he may change his look to fit in with the new group. More than likely, the boy more than likely will modify in some fashion what he talks about at the table, curbing it to match the given external environment of acceptance. Over time he may possibly manipulate how he talks to continue the social acceptance even further. He may change his thinking and his feelings to align with the group and what they consider entertainment and fun.

But perhaps the invitation was all a trick to embarrass him. Perhaps he is devastated and begins to find ways to avoid school. Perhaps he spends 15 minutes with the group but then later finds a group with similar interests. Perhaps nothing of note happens. The point is the battle between the boy's new external environment and his internal fears, discomfort or even excitement will likely impact his concrete beliefs in some way. But does it have to forever define the man he becomes? Regardless of the ending to his first day of school, does it have to end with a concrete belief that all things new are bad or scary or exciting? Did the environment influence him or did he influence his own beliefs or internal environment to assimilate to the external environment for acceptance or safety?

You create your now and you can reframe your past. Perhaps you could not control your past lifestyle, external environment, but as an adult you can control how you perceive it now. You are not just who you are, and it is not just what it is. It is what you make it. You experienced your life. You have changed tastes, likes and dislikes. You will likely continue to change these things. You were influenced but you can change your mind, your perception, your beliefs. You are not the same person you were five years ago, and you will not remain the same person you are five years from now. You are just growing. And if you are not growing by choice, be aware that everything in your external environment is changing. If you have stopped growing and simply have resigned to *this is just who I am*, be prepared to get left behind, because everyone you know, every place, everything in your life is changing, whether you recognize it or not, whether you acknowledge it or not.

But you don't have to be left behind. You know how you cultivated your present. You are learning how to cultivate your true self, your best self, free of old concrete ideas that are irrational. This is how you grow. Growth is a continuous state of change. If you are in a constant state of change, how can you ever just be who you are? You are simply what you have accepted to be true about you, as though you are frozen in time. But even frozen food has an expiration date; don't you think your old self has expired? You are presently the reflection of your perception of your life experiences and your chosen lifestyle.

> *Anything not growing is dead.*
> —Lauren Hill

Removing the label *that is just who I am* and having no label to replace it is uncomfortable. I mean it is *who you are* right? This society teaches you to define yourself by a lifestyle and a title or labels within that lifestyle. How do you know who you are? You already know that what we think and feel is based in concrete beliefs, beliefs that may have been passed down to you or conclusions that you came to from the culmination of small events or from some huge or horrible events. Maybe you don't even know where that concrete belief came from and that's OK. What matters is whether your beliefs are allowing you to grow or are holding you back.

One of the Components of Change that you need to evaluate is what part of your internal and external environments feel like real truth for you. Were you taught (directly and indirectly) that your value was in your accomplishments and performance? Were you taught that there must be evidence of your accomplishments in your lifestyle for you to have value as a person? This is bullshit. You are not on a performance-based contract with life. Your performance in anything does not determine your value as a person. Societal rankings and socially constructed successful performance does not determine your life's value.

Let's look at another construct for internal and external environments. Were you taught that your value was in making sacrifice for others? That your desires should be subjected to the needs of others, like your family or your religion or the company? Your value would be shown in how much you do for others, in how much time you spend taking care of everyone else, even strangers or how much time you spend at the company or at work. Caring more about others than you care for yourself is the measure of your value. You live a life in service to others, service that is so consuming it leaves little time for yourself or your family. Again, this is a performance-based value and when closely examined defies rationality.

First, let go of the sentence *that is just who I am*. This is an irrational statement on many levels, none of them good. It is not a statement of acceptance or self-love; it is a statement of surrender, of self-loathing or apathy. Do not let this sentence anchor you down any longer. It is such a surrendering concrete statement of self. You are also not your accomplishments, your performance, your lifestyle. Learn to separate your individual value from your performance. Most measures of self are merely social constructs derived from subjective notions accepted by a majority now considered to be the standard or worse, reality. There is a difference between personal acceptance, apathetic indifference and a blossoming self-awareness and an ever-expanding potential. Beware of forced contentment due to indifference disguised as self acceptance. You can be happy in the present and also reach for growth and optimization. These concepts are not mutually exclusive. In fact, living in the present moment as you grow in a positive way would be the beginning to my definition of contentment.

Your external environment shapes your internal environment and vice versa. This is not an argument for nature or for nurture, just my analysis to date. I believe they play off each other and you use each to shape what you choose to perceive either for safety, acceptance, or confirmation. Many times, you do not even notice you do it. Perhaps you simply refer to it as instinct, adaptation, or evolution. Agreed. Now you can evolve because with awareness comes change. Now you know you do it and how you do it. Your internal environment in a sense is like the weather. It can change suddenly and many times cannot be predicted. It differs from the weather in that you can control the weather of your internal environment.

Be careful when applying RSA directly to the lifestyle component. You need to remain humble and open and not be overly influenced by a strong desire you may have for a specific lifestyle. The Lifestyle Component to Change is not included in your I-to-E Inventory for this very reason. Simply apply RSA to the lifestyle component to cultivate a positive belief to keep you focused. Frame a new, positive and healthy lifestyle belief. When you cannot control the external environments, you can control your perception of them to control the emotional impact from any of it on you. If your environment is bad and you cannot change it, use it. Use it to drive you to work harder toward change. Stop using your perception to create it to be a handicap. It could be the best thing that ever happened to you. Change the perception and use it as motivation. Add your newly reframed belief to your LP and use it to refocus you when life happens and you become weary or discouraged.

Next, apply RSA directly to the People, Places and Things Components of Change which are included in the I-to-E Inventory. The ability to create actionable Purposeful Activities around these three subjects is rationale; however, they will also reflect the lifestyle beliefs in your LP. The people within your lifestyle tend to be more influential than the places and things, perhaps due to rewards like love and acceptance you perceive they give you. Dissect your concrete beliefs about the people, places and things currently in your life. Your newly framed lifestyle belief may have vaguely touched on these components. This time, more clearly define them in your lifestyle belief with more specific descriptions of the types of people, places and things that you will allow or include in your new life routine. Use positive adjectives to describe the types of people, places, and things you believe will help manifest your positive, healthy, and authentic lifestyle. These are not names of specific people, places and things, but descriptive of types of people, places and things. You will choose specifically during your I-to-E Inventory construction. Return to the RSA process map for a review of its application in a more detailed form if needed. Apply RSA to reveal three Belief Sentences to add to your LP about your lifestyle, including beliefs about the types of people, types of places, and types of things that you will allow in your new authentic lifestyle. Add the newly reframed, positive and rational beliefs about people, places and things to your LP just under your one or two sentence lifestyle advice.

Keep the Principles of Change in mind as you analyze your current beliefs about the people, places and things in your life. What do you really believe about these places and the things required to live this lifestyle and why? Look for subjective answers rooted in irrational concrete beliefs and negative perception. Question the discovered irrational and negative concrete beliefs using the basics of RSA, repeatedly asking *why* to all of your responses while paying attention to your thoughts and looking for the use of determinant words. *Why do I believe this clothing, these interests and that music make me who I am? Do they reinforce negative concrete beliefs about myself, others and the world? Why do I think these material items are who I am? Why do I identify with this group of people? Why do I believe this lifestyle has served me well? Why do I think this is what I want or what I deserve? Why do I believe these places and things help shape a positive outlook on my life?*

These are just a few examples of how far down the rabbit hole of your beliefs you need to travel using the RSA Tool of Change on each Component of Change. You are hunting for your innermost negative and/ or irrational concrete beliefs about your chosen people, places, fashion, music, housing, cars and all things in your present lifestyle. Most importantly, what negative and irrational perceptions are reinforcing beliefs that these people, places and things are who you are? Without them you would still be you. Analyze it all with utter humility, not naiveté. Do not just accept your thoughts as fact. Observe your body's reaction to thoughts. Find the concrete beliefs creating specific thoughts and question them thoroughly. Question it all.

Remember, what you think creates your current feelings and your behavior follows. No one person, group, place or thing is responsible for how you feel. I know it is hard to let go of that irrational concrete belief. By using RSA on each component of your lifestyle, you can reveal irrational dialogue that is blocking your ability to believe something different about the people, places and things that are a part of your current lifestyle. Remember, just because you think it or feel it, doesn't make it so. Your perceptions of truth become your life, your reality through your chosen rational or irrational self-talk, your dialogue, based in your concrete beliefs. This is what is creating the feelings toward any specific memory, person, place, or thing.

To summarize this portion: You will have applied RSA to the Lifestyle and to the People, Places and Things Components of Change in order to cultivate, at least four new positive concrete beliefs to add to your LP. Go ahead. Read aloud, from the top, your Life Philosophy to date. I'll wait. Sound like good advice? Of course it does; it's yours!

You will soon begin to remove and replace your external environments when you start your I-to-E Inventory, so be prepared for a total lifestyle renovation. You are currently renovating your entire internal environment. You are rewiring your internal environment authentically through multiple applications of RSA while in the process of revealing your authentic Life Philosophy. You are changing your thought processes on your own. Your I-to-E Inventory will help you cultivate your new authentic lifestyle in very specific ways, by creating Purposeful Activities around people, places and things that reflect your new LP. Be patient and kind to yourself, but take a no- tolerance policy with your own negative concrete beliefs. Your newly constructed internal environment will assist you in constructing your new authentic lifestyle from your truth, not your emotional needs. Your dueling internal and external environments will be no more. They will begin to work together because you are the master of both.

Trauma Implications:

If you have experienced trauma during your development years you may tend to *lose yourself* more quickly to environmental influence. You may be seeking safety, acceptance and confirmation to justify your right to exist. Innate desires to be loved and accepted (which you may have never felt) can cause you to use dialogue more quickly to justify your patterns of thinking, appearance and behavior, to more quickly obtain and retain acceptance. You may be allowing the external environment to shape your internal environment for perceived authentication based on emotional needs, not personal truth. This is forcing your chosen lifestyle to justify your individual experience and existence. This is living your inauthentic self. To cultivate your authentic self, you need to shed the inauthentic lifestyle.

Your Body Talks:

Your body informs you when you are living in-authentically. It will begin to inform you that your environments are not providing growth and may be leading you to destruction. This is one of the most amazing things about the body. It tells you when something is wrong! And it always wins! Pain can be seen this way at times as well. Physical and mental pain; the depression, anxiety and hopelessness you may feel is your mind and body screaming at you in unison *Something isn't right here! Get us out of here!* You may spend more frustrating time trying to quiet the body and mind rather than listening. Listen to your body when it is telling you your environments are dueling. Listen and observe. They will tell you when you are on the right path, and in the wrong place. Trust me, the people, places and things in your lifestyle give back.

You can't unlearn what you now know, and
you can learn that what you know,
is not everything there is to know.

CHAPTER 15

YOUR ROUTINES

You are what you repeatedly do.
- WILL DURANT

You may be one of those who fears routine; to you, it's just a synonym for rut. It's something that is imposed on you, that controls you. Or perhaps you just see it as boring or time-consuming. Remember, if this is what you believe about routines, then that is what it will be. Maintaining a routine can actually allow you more free time. For some it may be the beginning of balancing life. It will allow you to set aside time for personal growth work, time for new interests and more time with those you love.

Maybe you are the organized type; to you, it's a way of life. You consistently examine, order and execute your routines. But does your routine run you or do you run your routine? Do you live within your routine - experiencing life only through your daily regimen? Your routine controls you, so much that any interruption, any request to modify it, creates immediate stress and results in an instant *no, I can't.* Or do you use your routine as a guide instead of a gun? Are you willing to alter your routine given an opportunity to explore the experiences of new people, places and things; are you open to grab an opportunity to enjoy time for yourself or your children? Can you divert from your routine to experience new ways to think, feel and behave?

My point is many people, including myself at one time, prescribe a specific healthy routine for you. There is no doubt there is value in maintaining healthy routines in your life. But to tell someone exactly what their healthy routine *should* be, can be seen as irrational, especially if you are one who would be healthier with a little less routine or are someone who has never honored yourself with healthy routines. I like to hope the underlying intent of any of these *prescriptions* is really an offering of individuals' experiences of how they found their healthy routine and avoided pain and suffering. But I have yet to see a *one size fits all* daily, weekly or whatever routine.

People try other peoples' diets, they try to mirror the daily scheduling and processes of others and, often, these efforts fail or fade over time. Perhaps because these are not your Authentic Routines. They are not yours. Are they based on your true beliefs and revealed LP? Perhaps similar, but as the saying goes *Have you made it yours?* Is it filled with your wants and needs based in your new concrete beliefs? Or are these your awfulizing or musterbating? Does your current routine reflect your Life Philosophy and positive Core Beliefs?

The behavioral sciences tell us that routine is one of your strongest weapons for making change. There is truth in the old adage to *fake it till you make it.* But making it means achieving sustainable change. Sustainable change comes by fighting for it on four fronts: cognitively (The Principles and Tools of Change), biologically (genetic, sleep, nutrition, movement), environmentally (people, places and things) and behaviorally (Authentic Routine). The right routines, your routines, can reinforce success in each of these four fronts.

I know you have caught on by now. What do you believe about your current routine? What do you believe is a healthy routine and why? Why haven't you been able to sustain it? Apply RSA to your routine, your last Component of Change. What do you believe about routine and why? Do your beliefs about routine match your behavior, and more so your LP and all your advice about all the previous Components of Change?

Perhaps you think you have no routines. I suggest you just need to discover them. Explore your past, present and possible new routines. A healthy routine is usually both consistent and flexible. Consistency makes you strong; flexibility (for the right reasons) can help you grow. Both can keep you centered. When life happens, the job or relationship dissolves, you will be much more resilient. You develop, maintain and cultivate your Authentic Routines to live your Life Philosophy. It keeps you balanced while you continue to grow in competence, with enthusiasm for life. The foundation of your authentic and individualized routine can now be built on your new positive and rational beliefs about each of the Components of Change; sleep, nutrition, movement, mental and medical care if necessary, positive and authentic environments of inspiration, competence, connection and growth.

Your Authentic Routine is maintained and expanded by your daily choices, behaviors and experiences. You will soon be making positive daily choices with intended purpose, purpose and intent to balance and grow your mind and body. You will cultivate your purposefully Authentic Routine. A routine with purpose based in your truths, in your concrete beliefs. It will reflect the positive priorities you have chosen. It will also be based in your real life, which may include the care of young children or an aging parent, or the two jobs you are working to free yourself of burdensome debt or your plans to leave an abusive relationship. As such, you will control your routines; they will not control you. Your routines will support you, not drain you. If you sincerely desire the new positive change reflected in your LP but are constantly disappointed in yourself for failing, your new Authentic Routines will create the space you need to make progress, to develop the discipline to achieve them.

Where would you start? You would probably focus on your daily routine of nutrition and movement. You would focus on maintaining your mental and medical health and begin looking for new environments to build a new routine, right? Exactly! By basing your Authentic Routines on your new, positive concrete beliefs, your Life Philosophy, you will be a step ahead of life. Keeping a clear, rational and positive mind in your new beliefs allows you to maintain and even grow from those unexpected moments life throws at you, being fired from your job, left by your partner or betrayed by a friend will be painful and life-changing. But your routines will provide you stability while you stay rational in the face of your throbbing emotions.

Apply RSA to reveal and frame a new positive belief about routines to add to your LP. If you already have, read it aloud. Sound like something you believe in? Apply RSA even if you think you already have a positive belief and or routine at your core. You need to know literally what it is—each word of your positive concrete belief that is backing your positive thoughts and actions in maintaining your current routine. Go ahead; the next sentence will be here when you are done.

Your Tools of Change, RSA and your now complete LP Foundation will help you reduce emotional toil and inauthentic choices when filling your I-to-E Inventory, your final Tool of Change. This time you are properly and authentically mentally prepared for the behavioral battle. You are armed to make choices differently, practiced in processing life events, people, places and things more rationally. You are aware that you control the emotions. You are writing the narrative of your life with your thoughts and beliefs. You understand that you perceive your reality and shape or reframe your internal and external environments. You have built your routine, now rooted in your positive ideals and beliefs; it is not built on must or supposed to, it is not based on your performance or outcome. Your routine now reflects your authentic beliefs and your genuine aspirations.

When you organize your efforts based on your authentic beliefs, you begin to work life. Life stops working you. Your routine is where you begin to organize your efforts, your cognitive, biological, environmental, and behavioral efforts. I believe it takes an enthusiastic effort to concrete change in your life. You already have value. You've had that the entire time. Your Authentic Routine is designed by you, from your most positive and authentic Core Beliefs.

Once you have completed the installation of each of the Components of Change into your I-to-E Inventory, you can begin to tinker and eventually construct your Authentic Routine on a daily, weekly, monthly or yearly format. After all, it will be your healthy routine built on your humility, competence, experience, confidence and enthusiasm. Remember, they said you have the right to pursue happiness. I say you have the right to create it anytime, anywhere.

YOUR LIFE PHILOSOPHY FOUNDATION

Each sentence begins with "Remember ..... is rational, and ends optimistically.

Remember .....

The World _____
_____

Others _____
_____

Self _____
_____

Mentor/Quotes _____
Reframes _____
_____
_____
_____
_____

Nutrition _____
_____

Excercise _____
_____

Sleep _____
_____

Current Diagnosis _____
_____

Current Treatments _____
_____

Lifestyle _____
The Essence of _____
(non-specific) _____
People _____
_____

Places _____
_____

Things _____
_____

- Additional Belief _____
Sentences Derive from _____
applying RSA to any life _____
lesson, experience, _____
moment and/or _____
concrete belief _____

To use
**Simply recite your Life Philosophy
to remind, and advise yourself.**

COGNITIVI
RAMPAGI

There is no limit to the length of your Life Philosophy

PHASE V: CREATING YOUR CHANGE

CHAPTER 16

THE I-TO-E INVENTORY

Balance and routine are not passive.

You are on a mission to reveal your authentic self and create your authentic lifestyle, a life purposefully built with Purposeful Activities so you do not have to find purpose. Purpose will find you. Humbly excavating and examining your concrete beliefs, re-writing those beliefs with positive, rational themes, seeking authentic competence by questioning and searching yourself, others and the world to write your Life Philosophy (LP) is how you will cultivate your authentic self, and create and sustain happiness.

Your I-to-E Inventory will reveal specifically who, what and where will become a part of your Authentic Routine, *a routine consistent with Purposeful Activities practiced for personal growth, competence and experience.* Purposeful Activities: *any activities performed with the intended purpose to gain competence.* You will populate, grow and live your I-to-E Inventory with your Interests and Purposeful Activities, choices you will organize, practice and optimize within your Authentic Routine.

Do you remember a time when everything you could see, hear, taste, touch and smell was the most amazing thing you had ever experienced? If you can't remember, perhaps you have seen a child stare at their own hand with a look of amazement over and over again. Where did your curiosity go? You can't possibly have experienced everything there is to experience or know all there is to know in your brief human existence. So I ask you, where did the curious enthusiasm go? Your childhood gaze of amazement and wonder. *Ah to be a kid again* is usually followed by, *but only if I could know what I know now.* Well, you can live with enthusiastic curious again while also knowing what you know now. It takes the willingness to be uncomfortable. When you were a baby learning to walk, you struggled and fell countless times without ever knowing the freedom that awaited you. When you were learning to ride a bike, do you remember how afraid you were; how many times you fell? Maybe but do you remember how quickly that fear turned to joy when you found your balance and sped down the sidewalk? You persevered before you knew what perseverance was or what the reward for doing so would be. Be as a child. Challenge yourself to learn about yourself. Be willing to stand in the unknown, the constructively uncomfortable and smile with curiosity as you analyze your dialogue and ask a child's favorite question: *Why?*

As you become comfortable with a little discomfort, be open to the knowledge and experience of others. Humbly greet the thoughts, experiences and perceptions of others as an opportunity to see a new perspective and perhaps gain more competence. Enthusiastically practice humility to gain self-competence. Self-competence includes self-awareness. You can maintain a confident and genuine awareness by using rational observation and optimistic analysis of self, others and the world. Continue to challenge what you think and what you think you believe.

It is time you also challenge what you do. What you do can affect how you feel as often as how you feel affects what you do. Yes, your dialogue creates your feelings and your feelings push your behavior. Not only can you change your dialogue to change your feelings, but you can act or behave to overcome your feelings. You can choose to act against how you may feel or think you should behave. This is how your behavior can affect how you feel more than letting how you feel affect what you do. This means you now have two weapons to manage, control or overcome your feelings: how you think (cognitively) and how you act (behaviorally).

Let us be rational here. Not *all* humans can *always* respond in alignment with their concrete beliefs. Life gets the jump sometimes. Your immediate behavior can be your emergency hatch, your safety net. Imagine you are standing in front of your house; it's been a tough day and you are trying to regroup and get positive again. Suddenly, a very grumpy neighbor comes out front and begins yelling as he approaches you aggressively. You think to yourself, *This just isn't the day.* You (irrationally) choose not to use empathy, RSA, your LP or to do what you would advise. (By the way, that is a lot of chosen ignorance.) In fact, your feelings are telling you that you don't have to take this anymore, let all that frustration from the day loose; you've had all you can take. Instead of choosing the behavior your thoughts and feelings are pushing you toward at the moment, you choose to sprint a hundred yards in the other direction as fast as you possibly can. I know, I know. You don't want to look afraid. That's just pride fucking with you. Guess who is standing a hundred yards away from the toxic person and is too tired to care? Now you can use RSA, consult your LP, and ask what would advise the person you love most on your walk back. Maybe he will be done ranting and have gone back inside. If not? Yes, sprint again if necessary. Silver lining: the meaner the neighbor, the better shape you will be in. He may even laugh. Maybe you two will start training together. My point is you can choose a positive behavior that ignores your thoughts and feelings. Against most odds, you can still choose to act better. And remember, that sprint began with a thought anchored in a concrete belief that you had a hard time grabbing at the moment. The next time it happens, your thoughts may assist your behavior rather than fight it.

When your feelings or thoughts are trying to talk you into something that is inconsistent with your concrete beliefs, reach for action. Take the action you would want your feelings and thoughts to initiate, to support but for whatever reason, they are not doing their part. Whether it is getting in your workout or getting to bed at your chosen time or refusing to engage in judgment and criticism. Run (sometimes literally); the thoughts and feelings will follow.

Believe you are a moldable and pliable organism influenced by both the mental and physical. The best part is you can manipulate yourself and your environments to create and mold change quicker and more authentically. You control your life experiment with your choices and your behavior.

You are now armed with two highly effective Tools of Change: RSA and Your LP Foundation. You are about to build your final Tool of Change: your I-to-E Inventory. Applying RSA gives you direct passage to rational self-awareness and self-competence, awareness based on authentic revelation discerned with humility. You have now internally planted positive and rational belief seeds into each Component of Change, ready to be cultivated. Your beliefs about each of the Components of Change will produce authentic revelations through life action, action reinforced by a routine, purposefully structured to promote growth within the Components of Change. You will need to keep all the Principles of Change in mind and utilize and sharpen both of your Tools of Change to build your I-to-E Inventory Tool of Change. Your I-to-E Inventory will break your vicious cycle and end your linear journey. It will surely dose your human experience with authentic revelation.

Your I-to-E Inventory will place you regularly in new experiences guided by genuine interest discovered through self-analysis. It is your map to an Authentic Routine of perpetual revelation and optimization. Unlock the infinite possibility of turning your beliefs into experiences. Map your constructively uncomfortable opportunities for growth. Use this inventory to uncover areas in which you need or want to seek competence and/or experience. You may expose a passion. You will soon begin to humbly invite the constructively challenging experience and opposition of all kinds because you are learning to embrace being uncomfortable rather than being defensive or fearful.

Your I-to-E Inventory will help you organize and diversify your Authentic Routine with Purposeful Activities. Activities you have freely but purposefully chosen to pursue an interest, to elevate an existing interest to competence or to achieve greater confidence in something you are already competent in. Activities with a purpose in mind. I do not mean *purpose* in the sense of your life's meaning. Neither I nor anyone else can tell you your purpose, nor do I think you find purpose. I believe purpose finds you through purposeful structure and hits you during experiences in your lifetime. I think purpose can change. Purpose is wildly dynamic, but also misleading. Passion can be mistaken for purpose. I will close with more on the purpose myth in the last chapter.

Your chosen Purposeful Activities may, will, hopefully take you outside of your comfort zone. The best teaching experiences are usually life's most uncomfortable moments. Those moments that change a concrete belief immediately. If you grow most from your valleys, are they even valleys after all? Uncomfortable is where the change is. Be constructively uncomfortable in your Authentic Routine.

The Interests you identify in your I-to-E Inventory may ignite or may fizzle. But don't quit too soon! I encourage you to pursue an Interest until you have achieved some level of competence. That may be enough for you. But if you keep seeking competence, many times an excitement begins that bursts into passion. Passion is as fleeting as excitement. Passion needs to be fed with competence and experience. Without persistent experience, you cannot continue to function at an excited or enthusiastic level pursing your passion. You begin to lack excitement and persistence goes wayward. Pursuing Interests and passions by seeking competence leads to a confident enthusiasm and creates happiness, satisfaction with your life.

What if you were able to be enthusiastic about exploring and cultivating your authentic lifestyle? Imagine if your life was your passion. If each tomorrow felt like your birthday. How might you think, feel and behave? Nothing is stopping this from being your reality except you. The moment you drive toward change you begin to live in the optimistic possibility of your capabilities and the positive hope given by human potential. You can utilize all that life has to offer, not be focused on what life has not offered you. You can begin to break free from living in the pessimistic perceptions of your perceived reality. There is no natural existence pattern of peaks and valleys guaranteed in life. You just perceive there to be. To peak is to die. If you are still here, be excited for your potential. Your valleys made you. Be grateful for them. Happiness is a cultivated state. Change is constant; competence is key; humility is the door to authentic self-revelation.

The I-to-E Inventory is founded on the CCE Principle of Change. Competence to Confidence to Enthusiasm. Refer to the CCE chapter if necessary. It is short for a reason. Feeding interest and creating experiences leads to competence. Competence builds Confidence. Confidence feeds Enthusiasm. This is the I-to-E Inventory foundation.

You begin the I-to-E Inventory by exploring each Component of Change and your LP and answering the four I-to-E entry questions. Your answers to these four questions for each of the Components of Change and your LP are placed into your I-to-E Inventory.

To enter each of your Purposeful Activities into your I-to-E Inventory you will ask the four entry questions and relate them to the Component of

Change in question. Simply write in your one or more answers or Purposeful Activities into the I-to-E Inventory in the corresponding column and row locations. See the inventory diagram at the end of this chapter for a visual reference. I will elaborate on the four entry questions in the next chapters as they are configured specifically to the individual Components of Change.

You are going to consider your Life Philosophy and the Components of Change. You are going to quickly think about activities and experiences that interest you and are related to your LP for each component. You will rate these activities and experiences relative to your current level of knowledge and understanding:

The Four I-to-E Entry Questions

1. Are you interested in a certain activity, topic or experience but have little or no knowledge or experience with it? You place this activity or experience in the (I)nterest column.
2. Do you have minimal or basic understanding or competence in a specific activity, topic or experience but not enough to be authentically Confident? Then you would place this activity or experience in the (C)ompetence column.
3. Do you hold competence and experience to the point of genuine Confidence in the activity, topic or experience, but you lack the Enthusiasm in its practice? You will place this activity or experience in the (C)onfident column.
4. Finally, if you hold competence to the point of genuine and authentic Confidence and you enjoy it enthusiastically, then you will place your activity in the (E)nthusiastic column.

As you review the experiences, topics, activities and even people you list in your inventory, you can choose those that you will purposefully pursue. If it is an activity in your Interest column, you will begin by seeking basic competencies. If you place it in the Competence column, you will probably need to plan more experiences to gain additional competence. Your

Purposeful Activities in the Confidence column tell you that you may need to consider different types of experiences to cultivate Enthusiasm. Your Confidence column selections do not necessarily move to the Enthusiasm column. If your Confidence selections grow into paths to enthusiastic states, then move them forward to the Enthusiasm column. Confidence does not guarantee an Enthusiasm, but it produces experience, knowledge and wisdom. At a minimum, you will be confident it does not make you enthusiastic at this point. Knowing from experience is better than wondering *what if?* Your Purposeful Activities in the Enthusiastic column are your guaranteed go-to practices that bring you joy. Competence, experience, Confidence and Enthusiasm come together for you. In pursuing these activities and experiences, you create a state of happiness within yourself.

Simply filling out your I-to-E Inventory will reveal, remind and celebrate the fact that you hold certain competencies and point you to where you have the potential to spark new interests or achieve greater Confidence and Enthusiasm. Passions you may have never even thought you would or could have may suddenly appear or slowly reveal themselves. Be humble. Be open. And change your life in ways you never thought possible or even considered. Begin seeking genuine competence with an optimistic perception of the possibilities. Cultivate. Break the negative concrete beliefs with the practice of humility. Passionately beginning to seek self-competence will lead to self-confidence. Self-confidence creates an enthusiasm that will fuel a passion for your life and a more persistent state of happiness.

Your I-to-E Inventory will help you grow your Interests, expand and master your Competencies and feed an authentic and genuine enthusiastic Confidence. Continue to add new pursuits to your Interest column as previous selections empty into your competence column and become *Purposeful Activities*. This is exploring yourself, others and the world. Be aware; new and slight interests can quickly shoot to enthusiasm if you hit passion pay dirt. Trust that your journey will get quite exciting and revealing.

Your I to E Inventory

Componants to Change	Are you ... Interested → (no competence)	Competent → (few experiences)	Confident -x→ (fully competent)	Enthusiastic Makes you happy
Nutrition				
Movement				
Diagnosis Current & Professional				
Treatment				
Mentors - Primary Multiple				
Mentors - Virtual Multiple				
New People				
Current People				
New Places				
New Things				

Move your I.C.C. to the right until you have dismissed it, or are Enthusiastic

CHAPTER 17

BUILDING YOUR I-TO-E INVENTORY

Know thyself.
-DEBATED

Explore thyself.
-THOREAU

A s you prepare your I-to-E Inventory, keep one thing in mind. There are no wrong answers except the ones that don't fit you. You have already clarified your concrete beliefs about each of these components in your LP. This step is about finding Purposeful Activities that align with your concrete beliefs. If you get stuck, go back to your LP. Use RSA to re-examine your beliefs and perhaps restate them. Review the Principles of Change and the components chapters if needed. But don't forget to have fun!

You have begun your cognitive attack. Your internal charge to change. Now you will begin your behavioral charge. You will visit each of the Components of Change again, this time to fill in your I-to-E Inventory. Component theory regurgitation is limited here. This chapter's primary focus is for discovery, installation and application, not theoretical expla-nation. Refer to the Components of Change chapters to reference any theoretical notions behind nutrition, movement, sleep, environments and lifestyle design. You are about to get specific with your choices relating to these components. Remember to use RSA and your LP to help you ana-lyze, choose and continue to work your I-to-E Inventory.

If you are struggling with enjoying this process, perhaps it is because you feel you have failed so often in the past. Perhaps you fear you won't be able to create or sustain change. This can happen because you may have tried to force yourself into a regimen or program not in line with your Core Beliefs, your biology and perhaps even research. Or you simply may have not been genuinely interested. First, let me assure you that you never failed; you just learned how not to do it next time! There is no failure if there is learning or growth; more about this later.

You may have had to force these components, solely motivated by knowing you should. Not because you truly believe in the method(s). Belief congruency matters for sustainability as much as having the knowledge and experience. Your concrete beliefs hopefully reflect what you learned from those attempts to change. If not, then it might be time to go back and re-examine them, to apply RSA to what you already know about yourself and these components. When the efforts bring on more stress, guilt, regret and shame, it's time to re-examine your beliefs and/or your chosen activity; something is not aligned.

For example, use your newly cultivated positive beliefs (Your LP) about nutrition and movement to help you more accurately target potential interests within both the nutrition and movement Components of Change. These again are your answers to the four I-to-E entry questions. Again, these are your answers. Let the seeking out and putting into action your Purposeful Activities create the experiences that will solidify your new positive concrete beliefs about nutrition and movement over time. Or let those experiences help you fine tune your concrete beliefs to more accurately reflect who you are becoming.

I like to think there are no bad kissers. If two supposed bad kissers kissed, neither would perceive any such kiss to be bad; for them, it would be the best kiss they ever had.

There are so many options, paths and possibilities. You have to continue to chase experience by seeking Competence until you reveal the facets that energize, heal and literally move you. The ones that make you want to research, experiment and even share. If you believe you have *tried everything out there* and just believe something is *different or wrong with me*, you are right. You believe something is wrong with you. Nothing is wrong with you. You kiss just fine. You just have to find the nutritional and movement approaches that kiss you how you like to be kissed.

Part 1: Your Nutritional Pursuits

The foundation of health is your biological functioning. Health begins at your biological level. But you know this already. Your own philosophy backs up this belief. There are many programs, ideas, theories and methods that do work on some level and many that do not. Many nutritional methods that do provide change can also hurt you, outweighing the positive effects initially received overtime. Be diligent in your research, not just your personal experiences. It is about finding the nutritional methods backed by proven research that match up to your biology. Not personal opinion. Align your chosen nutritional answers with your positive Core Beliefs. Beliefs you are now aware of and have cultivated on paper. Not just because you know or think you should. Experience is the best teacher. Research and science is where to begin to build your competencies.

Nutrition is the first component you will install into your I-to-E Inventory. Refer to the illustration at the end of this chapter for a visual reference. You can write as many answers in each column as you like. Be as specific or as general as you want. You can go back and review and refine later. But remember to have fun. Remember the H=C Principle here; Humility brings Competence. Refresh yourself with this Principle of Change each time you ask yourself the questions. You begin the installation of each Component to Change by asking the four entry questions

1. Are you interested in a certain activity, topic or experience but have little or no knowledge or experience with it? You place this activity or experience in the (I)nterest column.

This can any nutritional aspect that has sparked even the slightest interest in you. Perhaps a friend you know has done well on something relating to nutrition that you find interesting, an ad you saw or even as small and specific as a single meal or recipe. This can also be as wide as an entire approach to eating such as the Mediterranean or Paleo approaches, a vegetarian or plant-based approach or something more meaty like the *Primal Blueprint* approach designed by Mark Sisson. Your answer could also be as small and specific as finding a healthy shake recipe, researching holistic or performance supplements, learning more about specific topics like ketosis, power foods or even organic farming. Take a cooking class. Because of your schedule, maybe you just want to learn to cook some quick, easy but healthy recipes. Just follow your nose. Consider even the smallest and slightest interest you may have hiding behind your *I don't know how.* Get out of your own way but remember, do not toil on any of these entry questions. Answer immediately. You need to pull from your initial beliefs, thoughts, experiences and wisdom (or lack thereof). Remember all of this is writable. Do not create stress. *I don't know* is an OK response as well. This informs you where you need to be hunting. Again, have fun as though this is one of those online quizzes or assessments many enjoy. The difference is this inventory is based in science. It can be anything you have a nutritional interest in learning about or experiencing. Place your answer(s) in the Nutrition row under the Interest column of your I-to-E Inventory. Your answers are unlimited for your Nutrition Component of Change. You will begin to create experiences by seeking competence in each of your answers. When you have obtained competence and experience with your Interests, move your answers to the Competence column. Your nutritional Interests or answers have now become Purposeful Activities.

2. Do you have minimal or basic understanding or Competence in a specific activity, topic or experience but not enough to be authentically Confident? Then you would place this activity or experience in the (C)ompetence column

Purposeful Activities placed in this column reflect those topics that you would not have a public debate on due to your lack of experience, but you can hold an intelligent conversation on the subject. Remember the H=C Principle here. Refresh yourself with this Principle of Change each time you ask the four I-to-E Inventory Entry Questions. Your answers placed in the Competence column are already considered Purposeful Activities. As I stated before, if you struggle to find answers for this and the next questions it is perfectly OK. Again, do not toil on these questions. This tells you where you need to expand your horizons. You now know where you need to seek competence and experience immediately. This also means your first nutritional Interests will grow quickly to the Competence column. Add new answers to your Interest column the minute you move one to the Competence column. If you hold a basic competence in any nutritional activities, add them in this column as well. Examine your answers for those that align with your LP. Look for areas where there is potential for it to move from the Competence column to the Confidence column. Perhaps a few more experiences can move them to Confidence column? The same goes for each of the remaining columns.

3. Do you hold Competence and experience to the point of genuine Confidence in the activity, topic or experience, but you lack the Enthusiasm in its practice? You will place this activity or experience in the (C)onfident column.

Do you possess full competency and extensive experience to the point you hold a genuine confidence in the chosen Purposeful Activity? Would you have a public debate on this Purposeful Activity and can you can argue both sides? If you cannot argue both sides for and against, then you are not fully competent and cannot hold an authentic confidence. Let this be your barometer for every Component of Change placed in the confidence column. An authentic confidence is based in genuine and researched competence and extensive experience. But you knew that already. True competence cannot be based in Facebook articles with sources you have not fully vetted. As we know now, fake news is easy to create and easy to propagate. The opinion of someone you trust and respect is not sufficient; certainly not hearsay or group think. You must even question your own experiences and the experiences of others. It is not that these experiences never happened or are being purposely or arbitrarily altered. But we know what happens when feelings impact thinking and behavior and vice versa. The point is real competence comes from challenging all that you think you know and examining all sources for bias, intentional or unintentional. There is no perfect solution, no perfect argument because we change; knowledge changes. Like the old food pyramid, science takes what we know and turns it on its head sometimes. So being able to see the strengths and weaknesses, argue both sides of the debate is what give you true competence and ultimately true confidence that leads to enthusiasm.

If you already have confidence in an area of nutrition, you might use this column for nutritional ideas that might enhance or expand that confidence or perhaps even test or challenge it. Remember to pay attention to your level of enjoyment as you move through your Purposeful Activities. As you approach Competence and Confidence, you may feel excitement, that *can't get enough of it* feeling. These are all positive but may fade quickly. If they do, there is nothing wrong; you have not found the Purposeful Activity yet that gives you enthusiasm, contentment. Remember, you cannot presently create a state of Enthusiasm with any of your Purposeful Activities that you choose to place in the Interest, Competence or Confidence columns. Discovering these differences within you on your own will require the practice of humility. Challenge your concrete beliefs, your experiences, your perceptions and observe your dialogue for irrationalities. Sift through the opinion, pride, ego, emotional and intellectual rationalizations and break through your cognitive dissonances. Practice humility, follow your interests and grow your competencies. Learn yourself to know thy self. Be kind to yourself.

4. Finally, if you hold Competence to the point of genuine and authentic Confidence and you enjoy it enthusiastically, then you will place your activity in the (E)nthusiastic column.

Enthusiastic echoes you are genuinely competent and experienced to the point these Purposeful Activities come from an authentic confidence and given the right opportunity, you would teach someone or the world this Purposeful Activity. Insert any Purposeful Activity nutritionally related that you are enthusiastic about under the Enthusiasm column. These are your go-to's. The activities you will seek for a guaranteed feeding of enthusiastic happiness. There is minimal to no resistance to performing these chosen Purposeful Activities. These Purposeful Activities balance your new and uncomfortable Purposeful Activities by dosing you quickly with guaranteed enthusiastic experiences.

Remember, not being able to genuinely and authentically answer questions two through four is OK. That too is authentic. You will have now zeroed in and can specifically target your competence and experience acquisition activities. No one knows all there is to know about nutrition. More is revealed daily and there is so much left to discover, study and experience. You have so much ahead of you to learn and experience. This is the journey. Enjoy the nutritional ride. Work your nutritional pursuits regularly. Proper and persistent nutrition will blast you into a biological change that will change your entire life physically and mentally. Remove and add new choice answers or Purposeful Activities to your Nutrition portion of your I-to-E Inventory. Try new things. Chase competence and experiences as though your life depends on it. The vastness of the nutritional world awaits your cultivation and personal discovery. Begin your personal relationship with your body by beginning with your authentic nutritional pursuit of happiness.

Part 2: Your Movement Pursuits

Allow your Nutrition I-to-E Inventory experience to be the method of discernment for evaluating and imputing each of the remaining Components of Change. Clone the application to the Movement Component to Change to insert it into your I-to-E Inventory. These can be specific and general. Detailed workout programs or as simple as a walk or play, movement philosophies and even outdoor activities like hiking or kayaking, for example.

It doesn't have to be expensive or strenuous or time-consuming. It needs to be what you are interested in trying, what you have tried and now are looking for more knowledge or experiences. It can even be what you have been doing for decades but don't enjoy anymore.

Enter your Movement Component to Change into your I-to-E Inventory now. Ask the four entry questions and fill in the movement component row.

Perhaps you have each column in the Movement row filled in or at a minimum you have an interest or two lined up. Maybe you were full of competence and experienced confidence in a number of movement related Purposeful Activities. Maybe you finally realized you don't play football anymore and you don't have to break your joints and ligaments down with heavy weight anymore. Maybe that occasional walk on the beach or through the neighborhood can turn into weekly Purposeful Activity. Regardless of how you filled in the movement component, whatever you already know, you can't possibly know it all. The vastness of movement discoveries, research, and experiences awaits your revelation to competence, to confidence and perhaps to enthusiasm, waiting for you to exercise your authentic healthy moves.

The idea here is that you are in charge of what will be experienced. Healthy experiences create healthy beliefs, thoughts, feelings and behaviors. If I tell you what to try, it will not be your authentic interests taking your there. Too much bias from me already exists in this text. Refer to the entry of Nutrition into your I-to-E Inventory. Follow your interests. Expand your current exercise competencies and cultivate your confident enthusiasm for purposefully moving your body.

Part 3: Your Diagnosis and Treatment Pursuits

You are what you perceive yourself to be. Labels can help focus treatments but also create self-fulfilling prophecies that emerge from inauthentic thinking patterns.

If you do not have a current mental health diagnosis and/or are not receiving treatment of any kind from a trained professional, do not include the Diagnosis and Treatment Component in your I-to-E Inventory. Instead, I recommend you work with your physician or other practitioner on the results of your annual physical, including any biological, genetic and other medical testing results, to review results, any potential issues or possible predisposition markers. This includes any physiological changes you may beginning to experience, perhaps related to age, prescriptions or environment. This can help you more accurately target your Authentic Routine to be even more preventive, more pro-active. This will help you prevent or slow the onset of potential physical or mental illness that may seem inevitable.

If you do have a current mental health diagnosis, proceed with this portion under the guidance of a trained professional. Only a trained professional can confirm or change your current mental health diagnoses. If you are receiving mental or medical treatment, do not alter or cease any present treatment or prescribed regime without trained and professional assistance. If what you are doing is as healthy as you now know you can be, it makes you happy and it is working for you, please keep doing it. While it is awkward to use the term *enthusiastic* when you are dealing with mental health diagnosis or treatment, in the case of this Component of Change, it relates to your enthusiastic belief that the diagnosis is accurate and the treatment is progressing positively or even has been successful. If so, place your diagnoses and treatments in your Enthusiasm column. This confirmation will just optimize what is currently working for you while allowing for expansion of treatment possibilities.

Again, if you are professionally diagnosed and receiving treatment, any changes from your prescribed routine are to be done with professional care only. If you are not confident or enthusiastic about your diagnosis and/or treatment, consult your current practitioner, but please consult multiple opinions from multiple disciplines as well. Don't just question your diagnosis; seek diligently to find competence and experience beyond your present practitioner until you are confidently enthusiastic about your diagnosis. Put together a team of professionals with different views and approaches if necessary.

There are a few differences in entering the Diagnosis and Treatment Components of Change into the Inventory from the method you followed for the Nutrition and Movement components. Place your specific diagnosis in the column that corresponds with your answer. Are you interested, competent, confident, or enthusiastic about your diagnosis? This will point you to where competence or experience is needed immediately or help you to focus more on the Treatment Component to Change. The other empty spaces in the diagnosis row are for differential diagnoses you will cultivate with a trained professional. This is a diagnosis generally similar in traits and symptomatology to your current diagnosis. This helps practitioners eliminate other possible diagnosis enabling a more targeted treatment plan. By definition, differential diagnosing is the process of differentiating between two or more conditions that share similar signs or symptoms. Use that phrase with your chosen practitioner(s), *differential diagnoses*. Do not do this on your own with Dr. Google or Dr. WebMD. Trust me; if your practitioner is worth their salt, they will appreciate your efforts. Many practitioners love to teach.

For the Treatment Component to Change, Purposeful Activities would include seeking competence and eventual experience in other possible and effective treatment options. There are a vast number of treatment approaches for most mental and medical health diagnoses that do not require synthetic medication. Attempt to fill each space in the row with a treatment or intervention that has proven to be effective for your current diagnosis. Search for competence and experience aside from synthetic interventions. Consider all options. Begin or continue with the holistic practices in conjunction with any current or further synthetic treatments. Again, work with your current and new practitioner(s). Please seek multiple opinions from mental and medical health providers. When you seek competence, you can ask related questions to learn from their experience. Inform them of the mission you are on and tell them how you need their help. If any practitioner tells you this is not necessary or finds this to be too much, I suggest you find another qualified replacement immediately.

When you begin to search for competence in diagnosis and treatments, remember you must be able to argue both sides of the debate. You are not a doctor or mental health practitioner but you can understand the basis for the diagnosis and treatment you currently have and you can research and question it thoroughly, particularly if you are not confident. Remember, search to prove both sides of the argument; you do or do not have a diagnosis. Seek multiple opinions and be cautious of any practitioner immediately wanting to push pills or perform a procedure. They both are a risk to your life. If your answer is that you are enthusiastic about your diagnosis, it would mean you are competent and experienced to a point of being confident that you are enthusiastic in treating the diagnosis currently affecting you. Remember, you are not your diagnosis. You are being affected by this diagnosis. You don't say I am headache do you? You can fight what is currently affecting you. You can heal and overcome most mental health diagnoses. You can believe that.

Part 4: Your People, Places and Things

It is time to evaluate the people, places and things in your life that are not consistent with your beliefs and your Life Philosophy (LP). There are probably needed changes that are obvious to you; you've always known these were not positive influences in your life. That was reinforced as you wrote your LP. But there may also be some people, places and things with negative influences that are more subtle but nonetheless unhealthy. Maybe the place has been a part of your life for so long, you have never considered its influence on you. Maybe some people have been a part of your life for so long, you have never really thought about the impact they have on you. Are these people, places and things positive, uplifting or inspiring? Do they reinforce your LP? Do you trust the advice of people in your life because they live a life that proves they are worthy and wise? Or do you seek their advice because it perpetuates your stagnation; it keeps your life comfortable?

You spent significant time examining, evaluating and cleaning your internal environment. You have identified specific areas you want to focus on for internal changes. Remember, the external is not who you are. Your clothes, music, hairstyle and lifestyle are not who you are. These are things and accessories to you, not who you are. But, if chosen poorly, they can impact how you grow, if you grow and who you become. The tremendous courage you have shown to change your life needs to be supported by your external environment. That's why you need to be willing to purge it, all of it if necessary. Now is the time to make those tough cuts from your external environment that I told you were coming. Liquidate to return to what matters most. The core of you matters most at this point. It is time to shed any part of your lifestyle that is cancerous—all of it, even the 0.01%, even if you do not think it is relevant. Make anything, anyone and any place that does not support your LP, earn its way back to you.

If your LP and using RSA is not enough to help you decide who, what and where need to be removed entirely from your life routine, apply my *Rule of Two* to help you decide. The Rule of Two is for total life reconstruction and states that if any person, place or thing is two removed from a person, place, or thing you know is negative, they are cut from your life routine entirely. If your friend Bob is friends with a target you know needs to be removed, Bob goes, too, even if he does not live as the target does. And Bob's cousin. You do not owe them an explanation. This is not to say Bob and his cousin cannot return one day, but you are in life surgery, vulnerable to infection. You need to sterilize your operating room.

It all goes. Any place or thing remotely related to an infectious influence no longer exists to you. That song that puts you in the mood for going to that place on Friday nights you no longer go. The outfits you bought just for wearing on Friday nights to go meet those people. Hell, buy new dishes if you can afford it. Change your hair, buy that style of clothing that you've always said just isn't you. Have I lost you yet? If you cannot even let go of an outfit or a hairstyle, what makes you think you can change your life or push it beyond your comfort zone? If a style of clothing is too uncomfortable for you to try on, how do you recover from addiction or rise again from a divorce, job loss or trauma? If you find that letting go of these material markers is this difficult even in its essence, you may need to re-evaluate your beliefs, your LP. You may be trying to save your old life and leave yourself a *fuck it* exit. Changing fashion, hair and even your entire community isn't going to kill you. It will definitely make you uncomfortable. Think of it as a physical shedding of an old understanding of self, others and the world. Make it symbolic or ceremonial if you need to. Clear your entire lifestyle canvas if necessary. As Carl Jung might say, you are too susceptible to symbolism during a metaphoric life surgery.

You want to cultivate people, places and things that reinforce your positive concrete beliefs, your LP, your new routine and behaviors. Choose wisely, cut sharply. Find influences that offer support in your life; support with no connection to cancerous influences. Maybe you have a parent or sibling who knows some of the same people, but they do not associate with or live the negative lifestyle. A relationship with this parent or sibling would actually benefit you because they could model how to avoid infection from these people. But do not continue to see the people you are removing from your life; there is no excuse to be around them. Use RSA on any disputed external or internal environmental influence or support. Accept the answer at face value for life optimization.

As you begin to shed your old lifestyle—and jettison the people, places and things associated with it—it may feel like you are alone. Immediately apply RSA if these thoughts occur. Check and reframe the dialogue. You are seeking solitude to cultivate a more rational, optimistic and authentic self. You need no distractions or infectious influences. Do not worry; this will not last long. Your new and authentically cultivated internal environment and behaviors will begin to naturally create a new external environment based in authenticity, not circumstance or assumptions. You will begin to construct your new lifestyle with your new positive and rational beliefs. A new and authentic lifestyle will begin to emerge once you consistently begin to live your LP and work your I-to-E Inventory.

Now you will identify your *Purposeful People*. Ask yourself who are the people in your proximity and why do you allow them access to your life? What are their intentions for their life and does that align with your intentions for your life? Do they enhance or anchor you? Do they provide, feed and nurture you or do they bleed you dry? All these relationships will affect your life, even if they are not involved in your daily routine. They can indirectly stunt your growth or directly enhance you. It is your choice. You decide what people, places and things you will allow into your life.

Sections A & B: Virtual and Primary Mentors
On your list of Purposeful People, you need to identify mentors. Perhaps you already have some in your life. You may have had or may now have a sponsor, life coach, therapist, teacher or family member from whom you can learn and grow. Notice I did not say *friends*. Mentors walk a fine line. A friend is not a mentor in my opinion. Sure, we learn and grow with our friends, but a mentor is something different. You will define it with your personal truth. To me, mentors are people we choose for the specific purpose of enhancing our life learning and growing process. That means they are not there to be our friend but to be our teacher, our guide. When given the choice, a mentor will tell you what you need to hear, what you must

hear. If it is comfort you want, call a friend. If it is truth you seek, call your mentor.

Mentors are pivotal to your growth. Seek them out. Do not wait for someone to offer you. More than likely no one is going to ask you if you want to learn by giving up your time and pride in exchange for competence and experience. But this is precisely what you are looking to do! All you have to do is ask. It is very simple: *Would you consider mentoring me on your schedule if you have time?* Have a specific purpose in having them as your mentor; it can be helpful to clarify so that you both get the most out of your time together. You never know what can happen from simply asking. Jim Rohn says your time is your most valuable currency. I believe it is your time here with others and self that is your most valuable experience.

> *Experience is life's currency.*

You can have *Primary* and *Virtual Mentors*. Both terms have been used by Tim Ferriss, one of my most influential Virtual Mentors. Primary Mentors are those you interact with on a personal basis and from whom you receive personal feedback. Virtual Mentors are those you learn from through their works and platforms, books, talks, podcasts, interviews and blogs. You gain competence through their discussions about their beliefs, their perceptions, their experiences and by applying their principles. You might even be lucky enough to have brief interactions with your Virtual Mentors. Again, you never know what comes from asking, saying thank you or simply saying hello.

Mentors are generally more knowledgeable in areas of life then yourself. At a minimum, they hold more experience in a given subject than you may currently possess. They might simply live a life you respect or they have overcome tremendous hurdles. Through mentorship, you are given the opportunity to absorb the power of knowledge from others' experiences and discoveries. This will speed and enhance your learning, to reference a tiny portion of Tim Ferriss' amazing algorithm in his *4-Hour* trilogy of books. *Mentorship is faster competence acquisition.* I believe at its finest, received at your most humble hour.

> *One of the greatest values of mentors is the ability to see ahead what others cannot see and to help them navigate a course to their destination.*
> — JOHN C. MAXWELL

My brother taught me to contract out the competence you do not have but know you need. This is how you are to begin identifying and selecting your virtual and Primary Mentors. As you practice humility, you have identified areas of needed change, areas of interest or competence you want to gain. Who can feed your mind or even challenge your beliefs? Who will help feed your Cognitive Rampage? Whoever you choose, do not place them on a pedestal but do not become entitled either or confuse their role with friendship. Do not expect or make assumptions about them. They are human just like you, so don't be disappointed when they prove to be human. Ask questions if you can but listen more. Say *thank you* often. Talk about what you are learning with your family, friends and other mentors.

See one, do one, teach one is a powerful mantra in the medical field. A student wants to become a doctor but must first spend many years studying, hopefully from the best teachers. After some time in this role, the student becomes a resident at a hospital, where he or she spends hours and hours practicing to be a doctor under the watchful eye of experienced doctors and nurses. Finally, when the resident becomes a physician, the teaching of others begins. Perhaps teaching at a hospital, a university or even in their offices, teaching patients how to take care of themselves. But those doctors who excel, who become world renown for their skill or who develop new treatments, never stop the circle. They continue studying, they continue to observe and learn, experimenting and practicing with new ideas, even as they also teach. Apply this mantra to your life and actively seek mentors in your life; mental, physical and, yes, especially the spiritual mentors. Whatever that means to you. Enhance your essence, increase your competence, expand your experience and grow your confidence with the power of others' experiences and perceptions.

> *If I have seen further it is by standing on the shoulders of giants.*
> — ISAAC NEWTON

Your mentors can be good barometers for where your life is headed. Primary and Virtual Mentors will help you travel down your road of self-discovery and dose your daily life with competence and experience. Choose wisely, but give many a chance. Include mentors with views opposite your current views and opinions. You need to know both sides to be fully competent remember. Listen, learn and see one, do one, teach one.

The first people you will input into your I-to-E Inventory are Physical and Virtual Mentors. You know this is done by asking the four I-to-E questions which we will re-phrase slightly for clarity. Remember, you do not have to agree with the chosen mentor's ideals and beliefs; in fact, it is healthy to challenge and test your beliefs through exploration of opposing or alternate ideas.

1. Who do you have an interest in possibly being a mentor to you? Whose way of life, perceptions and philosophy am I interested in? You may not know much about them but there is something about their life or writings or podcast, etc. that interests (or challenges) you. Enter these in the (I)nterest column.

2. Who do you have some knowledge of (Competence) and think they might be a valuable mentor but you need to know more? You have read or heard some of their beliefs, philosophy and teachings but you need more information to know if it is a good fit for you. Enter these in the (C)ompetence column.

3. Who am I confident in as a Virtual Mentor? I am knowledge-able of this person's philosophy, teachings, beliefs, experiences and opinions. I trust their recommendations and use their ideas and approaches on a regular basis in my life. This mentor has

the potential to become one you are enthusiastic about but also may be one that continues in their current role in your life because of your confidence in them. Enter them in your (C)onfident column.

4. Who am I enthusiastic about as a mentor? Whose ideals, opinions, perceptions, actions and abilities do I share with others? Who I am enthusiastic in talking about and learning from? Remember, to be enthusiastic you must hold full Competence of the mentors' philosophies. Enter them in your (E)nthusiastic column.

Whoever you select as your virtual or personal mentors, keep feeding from their competence and experiences. At some point, you may discover they do not fit your LP. Or you may learn that your mentor is a charlatan who is more concerned with commercial success than living an authentic life. Or perhaps you placed them on a pedestal, and they fell, as all humans do. Whatever the challenge, do not immediately cease pursuing their mentorship. Uncomfortable is where the change is. This will only help you tune in even more to the values you hold dear and the philosophies you choose to live by.

You can have multiple mentors in all columns. Just do not leave a space blank. The objective is to fill in all spaces in this row. Add and remove Virtual and Physical Mentors whenever you choose. Choose carefully but keep your inventory filled with mentors at every level, especially Virtual Mentors. If someone sparks an interest virtually or in your proximity, add them to Your Inventory in the Interest column. If you think of someone or meet a person you think could be a Virtual or Primary Mentor, pursue their mind food with vigor before asking. Move (or remove) your mentors as you grow more Competent, Confident and possibly Enthusiastic in learning from them. Listen with a humble curiosity and do not assimilate their philosophies and beliefs without RSA and LP authentication. It is OK to challenge their philosophies, but humbly question yourself first. Mentors will accelerate your change, enhance your life, learning and growth.

Section C: New and Current People

As you begin to live your I-to-E Inventory and assimilate your Purposeful Activities into your Authentic Routine, you will organically travel to new places and do new things. This will inevitably introduce you to new people. You have RSA and your LP to filter these new people, places and things thoroughly before you decide to enter them into your I-to-E Inventory in the Interest column.

When you meet someone new, do not unveil your entire life story. Slowly share yourself as you learn who they are. Leo has always said, *Good relationships are about sharing yourself, not giving yourself.* RSA your own reactions to your new people and question all of your judgments, thoughts and feelings. When you meet someone new and they appear to be wired like you, place them in the Interest column of your Inventory in the New People Component row. Time will reveal whether or not this person can remain in your Authentic Routine. Again, you can add as many names as necessary in each column when exploring and expanding on any of the Components of Change. Do they make you better? Do they match your LP? Remember, when people show you who they really are, believe them. Once you have explored your interest in the new person and they remain in your life, they automatically become a person on your Current People inventory.

> *Become a student to others' perceptions, experiences, and philosophies while protecting and opening yours simultaneously.*

I saved the toughest part for last; your Current People. Remember, this is about saving your life, not theirs. You will be evaluating the people currently in your life and evaluating not where they belong in your I-to-E Inventory but if they belong there at all. After establishing your personal concrete beliefs and writing your LP, you may already know those in your life that need to be removed. Not only do they not fit in your LP, intentionally or not, they undermine it.

The reasons some of these people are in your life began with something you may now want to change. It can be the history between you that perpetuates your beliefs and maintains your perception that you need them or they need you. People connect in fears. If you and I were in a foxhole together taking machine-gun fire and we made it out alive, we are going to feel a very unique bond for the rest of our lives. Those in military service and law enforcement consider themselves bonded in a way that others cannot understand because they rely on each other for protection and sometimes for life. Maybe it was a life changing event that bonded you. Perhaps you both survived child abuse or abandonment. But if that person is not supporting you, not lifting you up, you may need to move beyond that bond of trauma. You are no longer taking machine-gun fire. You need to move forward; if they cannot move forward too, then model and live a new life. It may be exactly what they need to move forward to. But regardless, do not live in that history.

You may feel as though you can't let go of someone who is holding you back from living your LP because they are your only support system. But perhaps they are adding to your life's present weight more than they are helping you put it down? I know this sounds harsh, but I am trying to wake you up to acknowledge the importance of your own life first. Two drowning people cannot save each other. The point is you both will fall if you are not healthy enough to support your own weight, much less theirs. Imagine if you will a table, and you are one of the legs. The current people in your life are the other legs of your lifestyle table. If you are the only stable leg or you are as damaged as the legs around you; how sturdy and reliable is your table? If you have been leaning on these people and this lifestyle for support, this may explain why it held you up the way it has. Remember, be careful of your environments because they do give back. They are not you but they will influence you whether you like it or not.

As you consider who to place in your Current People Component, vigorously and unapologetically apply the Rule of Two. Filter these individuals not with compassion but rational thinking. With your truth, not emotion. Use your Tools of Change; RSA and Your LP to ward off historical emotional connections that were created by or are based in fear. Build an entirely new support system if necessary. You may find that no one can be placed in any column of your Current People row because they do not match your new life narrative or LP.

For the Current People Component, start with the last question first: *Who in my life am I Enthusiastic to be around and promotes growth in my life?* Now apply RSA and consult your LP as though your child's life hangs in the balance. Does this person remain in your enthusiastic column? Remember when I gave you Leo's advice: *When in doubt, do what you would advise.* Would you advise your child or closest loved one to hold on to this person? If so, add them to the proper column of your present understanding. If not, this is not the time for leniency.

Use all your tools as you evaluate the current people you choose to keep in your life. Move from those you are enthusiastic about, to those you are confident are a positive influence in your life, to those you want to know better or have an interest in knowing better, all because they support your LP. Perhaps they have different concrete beliefs, but they respect yours, perhaps they even challenge yours, but always in love. You know they always have your best interest at the heart of their advice because they live their own positive LP or because, like you, they are trying to.

Point of order. There are people in our life that we do not always choose. We cannot always choose who we work with or who is in our family. We can't choose our next-door neighbors or all the members of our team or the club we join. These are not the people that belong in your I-to-E Inventory. These are the people with whom we interact regularly or often. But they do not create our LP or influence how we live ours. If they do, then we need to apply RSA and determine why we have given this person such power in our life or why they may have been brought into our life. Perhaps they challenge us to grow more in love and tolerance. Perhaps they make us rethink our concrete beliefs. Perhaps these people challenge us to seek a new job or a new team or a new neighborhood, but that job or team or neighborhood will have others that we do not choose. And there will be people who do not choose us. Our LP will guide us as to how we live in this world with those we do not choose and who do not choose us but with whom we must interact every day, at work, at the grocery store, at the gas station. If we want a positive, uplifting life, the greatest challenge will come when we choose to live that way when there is no reward, no reinforcement. To the extent you can choose to surround yourself with positive people, places and things, do so! For the negative people, places and things, avoid them as much as reasonably possible. But when you can't avoid, choose to live your beliefs, choose to act on your LP. Let your life reflect your LP to those you did not choose but are, nonetheless, in your life.

Your chosen lifestyle, daily behaviors and the people, places, and things you assimilate into your Authentic Routine can greatly empower you. They can most certainly deconstruct you. It is time to save your life. Shed the weight of the past and its fears. Rise like the phoenix you are and lead your life. You were made powerful from the beginning.

Section D: Your New Places and Things

This is where you can allow your emotions and excitement to get the best of you. Your mentors will talk about places and things to do as well. Write them down even if they sound slightly interesting. The new people in your life may introduce you to new places and things. Even the current people in your life can provide you with opportunities, now that you have a mind-set to be open to them and infuse your LP with positive experiences.

Think of all the potential new places and things available to you in this world. Many are free to you. Add them to your Authentic Routine. Every leaf adds value to your life, every raindrop and every molecule of oxygen. Begin here. Begin by adding new places and things of inspiration that do not cost you a dime. Find yourself in nature as often as you can during your transition and throughout your journey of change. Clarity can be found in a simple stroll down the beach or a walk in the park. Invite others to join you, but learn to be alone in nature. Read and sleep alone under the stars at least once in your life. Spend as much of your life's currency with nature and those you love while you can. Your Spirit will thank you later.

Your New Places and Things do not have to be places and things in nature either. This is just my heavily biased suggestion. If you are avoiding it because it makes you uncomfortable, well? I suggest you also add places and things that positively enhance the social component of your life. Being around others and having fun is an important component of your Authentic Routine. Some of these will come through the new people and mentors in your life. But there are always those places and things that you have wanted to know more about, to learn about, to experience just for yourself. That is partly why the New Places and New Things Components of change have been included in your I-to-E Inventory. Follow the basic method and ask the four entry questions to add your New Places Component and your New Things Component to your I-to-E Inventory. Fill in as many spaces as you can. This will feed you many new experiences and point you in directions to where and what needs to be learned and experienced, as well as what and where needs to be removed as options to you. Filter all new places and things as you have done with all your previous choices and Purposeful Activities. Consider these your Purposeful Places and Things. Their purpose is to expand your life palette. Optimistically apply RSA, but do not forget what you now know. Your environments and the people, places, and things in them do give back.

Unbind yourself from impossibility or even improbability. This is not about goals. This is about aligning your Authentic Routine with your genuine interests, rational beliefs and wildest dreams. If you aim at a target 100 yards away and only move a millimeter to the right or left, how far off is your shot from the target? Living your Cognitive Rampage keeps you on target from the start and ensures you hit your mark time after time, no goals necessary. Input new places and things you want to discover and experience in your lifetime. Analyze whether they align with your LP. If they do not, adjust your aim. If they are sighted, then soon you will experience your dream place or thing. I bet it won't even be a thing.

CHAPTER 18

LIVING YOUR COGNITIVE RAMPAGE

Living your Cognitive Rampage has many definitions.

Living your Cognitive Rampage is humbly thinking, feeling and behaving as authentically as you can. At times, it may be easy. Other times, every hour may be a struggle. Some of this is growth. Some of this is you changing. To quote Tim Ferriss, *Ask yourself, am I having a mental breakdown or a breakthrough?* Your Cognitive Rampage at 20 will not be the same as your Cognitive Rampage at 40 or 60. That is absolutely perfect. You are absolutely perfect as long as you are authentically and humbly aligned with your beliefs. If you are humbly and earnestly pursuing your interests, seeking knowledge and gaining confidence and enthusiasm, if you are challenging yourself, if you are getting uncomfortable at times, you are living your Cognitive Rampage.

This process may change your beliefs. If it does, then you need to change with it. Re-examine the Principles of Change, the Components of Change with your new beliefs. Test your new beliefs with RSA. Being true to those new beliefs is as important as it was the first time through the process and it will continue to be important throughout your life.

Now that you have entered all of your Components of Change into your I-to-E Inventory, you can now complete the creation of your Authentic Routine. This requires you to schedule time for your Interests and Purposeful Activities. You can prioritize the component you want to focus on and the Purposeful Activities. You can try to do them all. The pace, the breadth and the depth with which you approach your Cognitive

Rampage is up to you. Build your Authentic Routine with your Purposeful Activities. Purposeful Activities routinely performed with the intended purpose of competence and experience acquisition. Apply all of the Tools of Change while remembering all the Principles of Change to grow and optimize all your Components of Change. Your choices just became literally purposeful. Your Authentic Routine will reveal your authentic lifestyle organically. Continue dosage as needed. Living your Authentic Routine is to live your Cognitive Rampage. Protect it and live it as though your life depends on it. It most certainly will grow from it.

Write down and outline your Authentic Routine. Remember, your Authentic Routine begins with your Sleep Routine. Before you go planning away all your energy, you first need to plan your sleep. Your Authentic Routine begins by scheduling your sleep and persistently protecting it.

The earliest and latest scheduled time in your Authentic Routine is the time you wake up and the time you lie down to sleep. Again, you cannot make up for sleep. An inconsistent sleep pattern will eventually spoil the efforts you are making. Your Sleep Routine is crucial. To be successful, you have to be willing to get sleep, not lose it. Protect it. Resting properly requires ingesting properly and consistently to ensure that you are doing all you can do. Synthetic sleep aids are not meant to be used for a lifetime.

You have documented your Nutrition and Movement beliefs in your LP. Be sure to include them in your Authentic Routine. Of course, there are holidays and special occasions; enjoy them! Just don't extend them! In the beginning, I recommend you schedule your Nutrition and Movement Purposeful Activities in your Authentic Routine to ensure they don't get lost in your old lifestyle and busyness.

Sleep: check. Nutrition: check. Movement: check. Of course, don't forget to schedule any treatments your currently participate in, whether this is physical therapy, testing, medical follow-ups, counseling, religious or social support functions. If you have added Purposeful Activities like getting an annual physical or investigating alternative diagnosis or treatment options, schedule them with your practitioners. Maintaining a persistent and continued drive to optimize your physical and mental health by including these in your Authentic Routine will generate tremendous returns for you, ones you may not be able to imagine right now. That is my prognosis for applying your Cognitive Rampage to your life.

Sleep: scheduled. Nutritional action: organized. Movement component: scheduled, exercised. Mental and medical fronts: treated, maintained and being pursued toward optimization or discharge. Your I-to-E Inventory is complete and you have plans to ensure the people, places and things in your life align with LP. Mix your time with your loved ones, friends and personal time into your Purposeful Activities. Learn to enjoy being still; learn to enjoy being alone. These too are purposeful. Begin your daily routine with five or ten minutes of simple scheduling. Pick one Purposeful Activity from each Component to Change in your I-to-E Inventory and place it in your Authentic Routine. It doesn't take long to go through your schedule and include Purposeful Activities or Purposeful People. These should be the things that give you joy. They should not be burdens or boxes to check off on your to-do list. If that is the case, repeat the process, eliminating any activities or people that are there because you thought they should be. Review your concrete beliefs and your LP; then use RSA to look at your inventory. Keep refining, keep honing in on the target until you have cultivated the answers, the activities that will bring you happiness and joy. You can enhance the lives of those around you by growing yours.

Your I-to-E Inventory is your pantry of goodies, your cookie jar of what to do, a blueprint to your authentic change, the answer for what to do, your path and philosophy to change, sustained growth, enthusiasm and freedom. It is a dose of authentic revelation. Look inside you for what you need. Let it pour out of you. You have always had what you need. You. Until you know who you really are, you need to make sure others and the world cannot fool you. People are not your source. Places and things are not your source. They are resources. They add to your essence. Your belief is your source. Cultivate it and define it in the essence of each of your days.

Tailor the Cognitive Rampage Approach as you apply the Principles, Tools and Components of Change. Stay humble. Continue to challenge what you believe as you feed your growing competencies. Don't fear new experiences. At a minimum, you will be able to say from experience that something truly isn't your cup of tea. Trying and knowing is better than not trying and continuing to wonder *what if?* Short-term pain versus long-term pain. Follow even your slightest interests as they emerge and feed them with competence daily. Force yourself to be uncomfortable searching for competence. This is how you will create experiences with intended purpose. In these experiences, moments will occur, life-changing moments, moments of revealed passion not known as they were restricted from emerging by your negative concrete beliefs. Through self-reflection you gain self-competence. This builds to your self-confidence, genuine self-confidence based in authenticity, not pride and emotional defenses and exaggerated excitement. Respect the process so you can enjoy the journey.

Focus on the fundamentals of the Cognitive Rampage Approach as you pour your Spiritual Rampage to mold your Cognitive Rampage; consistent practice of the Principles of Change; a humbled and intensive curiosity filtered by Rational Self-Analysis as you cultivate and live your Life Philosophy, gain self-awareness and understanding through regular competence collecting and purposefully structured behaviors to maintain and grow your Authentic Routine and lifestyle. These are the tools for creating life changes and life optimization. This is your Cognitive Rampage!

You will create this change right now. Open to the possibility that, even at its smallest, intrinsic shine can explode the darkest of times. It can explode in a fiery rage as though you are rampaging against the dark shouting, *I WILL NOT GO QUIETLY INTO THE DARK NIGHT!* Rampage for your life right now. Create your moments. Do not wait for them. Release the optimistic rage as though you are starving for your very next second of life. Remember to embrace every given moment of life with gratitude. Remember, if you now see the dark, it is only because you have also felt light. You are to shine in full display. It truly is the darkness you experience that makes you so special. You choose to stay in your darkness, or you choose to disburse your light. This is my philosophy.

If no one is in your corner presently, then please allow me to offer a cheering voice of loving optimism saying repeatedly to you, *Believe in the power of you. You are a superhero!* This is to Cognitively Rampage. To rampage is to destroy things around you or simply move and shake things up, a thinking rampage, a destruction of all existing irrational notions of truth and reality while mindfully observing, exploring and revealing the authentic self, done by humbly and enthusiastically questioning the world, others, and self with a humbled curiosity for competence, cultivating a passion for life by creating life experiences. This is to live a Cognitive Rampage. You can create your heaven on earth. Your redemption day is today.

CHAPTER 19

THE PURPOSE MYTH

You don't have to find purpose, purpose finds
you through purposeful structure.

How many times have you heard *Find your purpose and you will be happy.* As you may have noticed throughout this book, I have some issues with the notion of finding purpose to be happy. In fact, I say, *There is no purpose and you don't find it.* I know it doesn't sound romantic or motivationally inspiring. But insisting that we all have a purpose that we must find or we will have an empty and unfulfilled life is a heavy burden of irrational beliefs and perceptions. It is Musterbation at work.

So let me lift your burden and free you from the irrational belief that life is perfect when you have found your purpose. And if you don't find your purpose, well, you missed your chance at happiness and will now live forever unfulfilled, consumed with guilt and regret. This just isn't true. As if anyone actually knows their purpose and can prove it. There is no purpose light that flashes when you have *found your purpose.* No balloons drop when you think you've found it. And if you think you've found it, just wait. There is no perfect life and there is no perfect purpose. We may think we know what our life was meant to be but it seldom works out that way. And if it does work out that way, it is seldom as perfect as we thought it would be.

By now you know as well as I do that a single moment can destroy any perception. A once concrete belief can be suddenly cracked with doubt. That belief may be altered or even replaced with a new one, sometimes almost immediately. The old belief is gone and a new belief replaces it based on new knowledge or different experiences.

Where did we get the belief that we all have a purpose and must find it to be happy? There is certainly no rational basis for this belief; no scientific evidence or even psychological theory to base this on. There are certainly people who give personal testimony to the belief that they have found their purpose or who seem to fit perfectly with the work they do. But is this evidence that we all have a purpose and we need to find it? Is being good at something evidence that you have found your purpose? Is the level of your commitment evidence of your purpose? What happens if you believe you have found it, you follow it and it does not work out as you planned? Have you failed at your purpose?

Many times, being rational is mistaken for being negative. Taking the definition of purpose would assume that a persons' purpose is a singular objective and this one gift must be found, as if it is hiding from you. To tell people to simply find their purpose and they will be happy can be dangerous and destructive. Convincing someone that they have a pre-programmed purpose removes personal responsibility. They simply have to *find it*, not create it. Let us assume they set out to find their mysterious purpose; they don't know what to look for but they assume they will know it, feel it when they find it. But it is all to no avail. Perhaps they begin to believe that something must be wrong with them because they cannot seem to find their purpose in anything. In the end, they spend their time searching for something that they are supposed to have (purpose) but cannot find. It is a cruel errand they have been sent on.

But here is how you use purpose to your rational advantage. The notion of purpose is powerful, but it is not rational to believe it is one thing, that it exists but is hidden from us and we must search until we find it. But the concept also does not capture the full power of what this means and can do for you. Since you now know the idea of purpose is subjective and that it evolves, you know now that you have the power to deem something, many things a purpose. Do this to transform beliefs, thoughts, feelings and behaviors. You can create a purpose to complete an objective or many objectives that are important to you. This can begin with your vision. They can be huge challenges or small victories. These become your purpose because they are essential to you. We all know that life changes in predictable and unpredictable ways. Whether we are raising children, fighting cancer or trying to get a job, our purpose changes. That is purpose. Rational Purpose. No matter what you are doing, you are living a purposeful life already. You can believe that. I believe purpose is created and cultivated as we shape our talents to help other people, not ourselves.

NOTE FROM THE AUTHOR

Thank you to all that have supported and continue to challenge me. Thank you for making me better. Thank you for caring enough to say something. Thank you to my readers and listeners. Thank you for taking this journey with me and taking a chance on yourself. If any of this resonated with you, know it was not me. It was you. You did the hard part, you listened. Without that, this is just words and noise. Now go live YOUR COGNITIVE RAMPAGE!

Love you!
Adam Lowery -52

Remember, uncomfortable is where the change is!

PS: You can go to www.adamlowery.com and download for free all the illustrations found within this book. I hope you're taking care of you and now living your Cognitive Rampage!

ABOUT THE AUTHOR

My name is Adam Lowery. I am a Mental Health Counselor, Author, Host of The Cognitive Rampage Podcast and a Mental Trainer. I also take an activist role in treatment reform. I founded the diagnosis *Athletes Depression*, and the integrative psychological approach Transrational Structural Behavior Theory (TSBT). In my heart I am a father, son, friend and humanitarian. In my spirit I am a teacher and protector.

Through a violent childhood my only focus was my dream to play Pro Football. A college injury ended my NFL dreams. Angry, I chose a life of drug dealing that soon entwined with addiction. I transitioned to the nightclub business a saw quick success, but addiction followed. I kept it masked by money and parties. One night after a random sixteen hour life contemplation session I left my career, gave away all my things, left my four year relationship and friends behind and embarked on walkabout or what I call my *Spiritual Rampage*.

For 2 years I wandered from the Florida Keys to Tennessee, even a First Nation Reservation in New Mexico. I returned home a man on a mission to change self and help others do the same. Within 3 years I completed 2 degrees, published The Cognitive Rampage, launched a top podcast and founded the Athletes Depression diagnosis. I Cognitively Rampage (Speak) on all things mental health, social issues connected to mental health and athlete specific related mental health. I specialize in high performance athlete mental training and recovery.

In my flow time you will find me outdoors. I surf, dive, spearfish, kayak, offshore fish, hunt and have survived on a deserted island. If nature isn't calling, reggae concerts, music festivals or home talking with my daughter. I have a serious addiction to podcasts, competence, new experiences and randomness. I talk to strangers, and too much. I love everybody, including you.

Made in the USA
San Bernardino, CA
21 July 2017